About the Author

You have to find humour in the darkness. Janine Davis is always striving for her next adventure. At fifty years old, she is not finished learning and trying to grow in her spiritual self. She has still got shit to do! No time for slippers and soap operas. She is only looking forward to the next chapter and the joys it brings in the journey.

To the best client a P.T. could ask for stay strong ☺ Janine 2023

Janine the Machine

Janine Davis

Janine the Machine

Olympia Publishers
London

www.olympiapublishers.com
OLYMPIA PAPERBACK EDITION

A CIP catalogue record for this title is
available from the British Library.

ISBN: 978-1-80439-225-6

This a work of creative nonfiction.

The events are portrayed to the best of the author's memory, while all
the stories in this book are true; some names have been changed to
protect the privacy of the people involved.

First Published in 2023

Olympia Publishers
Tallis House
2 Tallis Street
London
EC4Y 0AB

Printed in Great Britain

Dedication

I dedicate this to all the women and men who are caught up in abusive relationships and think there is no way out. See the light and find your strength.

Acknowledgements

I would like to thank Stephanie Thorne, Rebecca Pullan and Emma Hills for your support in helping me to believe that I should tell this story. I would also like to thank Dan Hogan in making me believe I am worthy enough as a writer and third Floor publishing at Bournemouth University. Guys, don't think; just do and believe.

When you see that angry teenager or child that is difficult, ask the question: What is going on in their life that is making them act that way?

Before you write them off and tell them they will amount to nothing, ask them: Are they OK? You will not get the response you want first time round because their anger is the only way to survive the situation they are in. They will dismiss you. They will have an attitude that you will not care for. They will be obnoxious.

Show them that you care. Do not judge them. Build their trust. They have to believe that there is someone that honestly gives a shit about them.

The Office for National Statistics (03/2020) states that the stats for child abuse are: one in five adults aged eighteen to seventy-four years old has experienced some form of child abuse – emotional, physical, or sexual – or has witnessed domestic violence or abuse before the age of sixteen.

The systems that are in place to protect the children do not work. A bold statement, I know, but I have been in that system. I know all too well that they do not work.

When you grow up surrounded by dysfunction, how are you meant to make the right choices in finding your way out of the shit pool that has been introduced to you at such a young age?

How do you deal with the trauma of abuse? If you do not have the right pathways around you, you will turn to drugs, alcohol, eating disorders and crime.

I can tell you the cycle of behaviour that you repeat because you do not know any different about being loved. You are so desperate to be loved that you will fall for anyone that pays you the slightest bit of attention. You miss all the warning signs that will be there right from the beginning because it all seems normal to you. It is what you have grown up in. Before you know it, your self-esteem and who you are as a person is being taken apart bit

11

by bit until you think there is no way out and you are not good enough for anything or anyone.

The cycle of abuse just keeps repeating itself until you see the light and find the strength to get out and start loving yourself.

Part of the following story is not a defamation of character. I am not here to demonise this person. If you took away the alcohol, the steroids and the recreational drug use there was a caring good person in there. He just didn't love himself enough to not want to do all of those substances.

You often hear, 'I'm a happy drunk. I'm not an asshole.'

Let me tell you what you are when you drink. You are an asshole, even if you think you are a happy drunk. I have done enough nights on the door as security and lived with an alcoholic for eleven years. I know how people are. I include myself in that too. I think I am a stand-up comedian when I drink. I'm not. I'm just an asshole that is drunk.

Living with addiction is a tough road to take. Lies, deceit and the utmost selfish behaviour are at the forefront of the battle.

I was asked the other day if the writing has helped me. Can I now just move on and leave it all in the past?

Do you ever leave trauma in the past? Once you are in a place to be able to process that trauma, you learn to cope with the baggage it has left you with. You never just leave it in the past. It moulds you. Unfortunately, it makes you who you are as a person. You either come out the other side stronger, or you live a life on self-medication.

This is my story after winning a World Title in Thai boxing. I had finally made it. I had become someone. Life was meant to change. I had finished with the drugs and the drinking. I was striving for a better life. I had met Scott though. I thought he was a recovering alcoholic. I wanted to support him and be there for him. Scott had different plans.

Surplus to Requirements

I was at home feeling very sorry for myself. My right knee was absolutely fucked. A complete rupture of my ACL and massive meniscus tear. There was no way I could think about doing the second World Title fight that was set up for me at the York Hall four weeks after the first. In my deluded mind I did try to think if I could get around it. Strap my knee up or something. The mind of an athlete. Go figure. Any other normal human being would think 'No way.' I'm sat there thinking of ways around trying to get the fight done on one leg.

I had a phone call probably two or three weeks after the World Title fight.

'J, get yourself down to the gym!'

'I can't fight!'

'Get yourself down to the gym. Tom has brought over a load of Norwegian fighters.'

'I can't fight.'

Dave wasn't listening. 'Just get yourself down the gym!'

Tom had left The Bulldog and set up his own gym in Norway. He would bring over different teams of fighters to the UK for training at The Bulldog.

I got myself together, and did as I was told. Took myself off down to the gym. When I arrived, the gym was really busy. There were trainers and fighters everywhere. There were men and women all kitted up with gloves, shin guards and gum shields all ready to fight. They all looked like they meant business.

Dave said, 'Get your kit on!'

In my head I was like, 'Fuck, I've got one leg! I don't want to let anyone down. Dave has not listened to anything I have said.'

I was still working at the gym and needed to keep working. I was not in a position to let that go. I should have refused. But if I had done that at the time, I potentially would have been without a job.

I got my kit on. Strapped up my knee. I just got on with it. He paired me with this woman, a little taller than me, probably around the same weight. Dave always put me with women that were heavier than me to fight. I don't remember her name. She was gunning for me. She had been told I had just won the World Title and wanted to make a point of putting me in my place. Little did she know that I was fighting her with one good leg. I managed to stay out of trouble until she decided to do an axe kick to the top of my head. I was not wearing a head guard and this bitch, in order to make herself feel better, decided to drop her heel with full power to the top of my skull. What a cunt! I was so angry. But I couldn't respond. I was barely able to move about because of my knee.

At the end of the round, she came over to me and said 'So, you're a world champion?' She laughed and sauntered off like she had some kind of victory over me.

I was so angry, I had to go outside the gym into the stairwell because I was struggling to keep my emotions intact. I started to cry, not because I was upset, but because I was so full of rage. I didn't want anyone to see I was in such a state. Fuck, Dave had pulled me down there for himself. He did not think about looking after me at any point. I was put on show, like a fucking dancing monkey with half my fucking leg hanging off.

I stood out in that damp stairwell with some other dude. I think he was from the Norway camp. He looked at me with surprise and asked if I was OK. I didn't respond. I pulled myself together and I went back inside the gym. Dave decided to put me in the ring with another woman. She was definitely bigger than me. This time just boxing. I thought, 'Fuck this and fuck you lot.' I had a good round and almost knocked the bitch out. I got out of the gym quick smart and took myself home. I knew then that I was surplus to requirements. I wasn't part of a team. I was only useful if I could fight. That's when my relationship with Dave had started to take a turn. I didn't discuss this with anyone. I kept it all to myself, but I was awake and observing Dave's behaviour towards me.

I was at home one day and remember looking at my legs in the full-length mirror and being horrified to see that my right leg had completely shrunk. I couldn't stop staring at it. I thought, 'Oh, my God! I am going to be deformed for the rest of my life.' Muscly left leg, twig leg for the right. I mean there was a six-centimetre difference in size between both legs. 'Shit,' I thought, 'I have got to do something about this! Get into the gym and slowly start to build the size back up again, depending on the pain.'

At that time, and even now, people will always have an opinion. You will always hear, 'Don't do this, don't do that.' My school of thought is: Fuck you. I know my body better than anyone else. I will crack on and see how it goes. I'll listen to the pain and if there is no pain I will continue. If you listen to everyone in your life telling you not to do anything, you will never get anything done. You learn by your own mistakes. Crack on!

At the time, I was living with Scott, who I knew was an

alcoholic. Well, a recovering alcoholic. He had been through AA just before I met him. Scott had a tattoo on the underside of his left arm stating the date of his AA journey – 18/08/2002 AA. I'm not sure if it was the date that he started, or the date that he finished. I took it as his date that he finished. I took it that he was working on his recovery. I wanted to support him. The least I could do for him was not drink at all whilst I was with him. Isn't that the least you can do for someone that is struggling with addiction? I thought that tattoo meant something to him. A reminder of what it was he was trying to fight. The addiction to vodka.

It wasn't long after we had moved in that we were fighting. The flat we were in was based in the top end of Bournemouth, The West Cliff. Literally ten minutes away from Bournemouth Beach. More towards the posher end of town. It was the first time in forever that I had been given the opportunity to live in such a nice flat. A client had shown me her flat that she had for rent. Two bedrooms, massive lounge, bathroom, with a bath and a big kitchen. Under floor heating too. Sounds nice, doesn't it? Cosy warm feet. Let me tell you something about underfloor heating: it cost a fucking fortune to run! The whole place went round in a big square, you could run circles through all the rooms. When me and Scott were getting on, we would play fight and chase each other round in circles in the flat.

My client conducted six-monthly inspections to make sure the flat was being kept nice and tidy. I would slave to keep the flat clean. On one of the occasions, I had to put a towel over one of the doors. Scott, in a rage one night after one of our ever-occurring arguments that we were having, had punched a hole in the door. He didn't care. I tried to fix the door. It wasn't ours. I filled it with plaster filler and painted over it. It looked shit but it was the best I could do. Really, the door needed replacing, not filled with putty filler. I was mortified. I managed to keep it from them and from everyone else that was coming round.

In amongst the drinking there were tiny snippets of goodness. Scott was intelligent. He possessed zero common sense. He was well read. We would have great conversations about all kinds of topics: politics, art, books, music, films. Oh my god! Scott and films. He was obsessed with films. His mother dropped off boxes of his stuff to get rid of it out of her house. The boxes were just dumped and left. I knew he wasn't going to sort it. So, I started to sort through it to arrange where I was going to store it. The boxes were filled with reams and reams and reams of drawings of Sylvester Stallone and paper after paper of star ratings for films. The films were listed in chronological order. They would have star ratings next to them ranging from two to five. There was an obsessive application to both of these subjects. I say we talked about music. I talked about music. I have a very eclectic range of what I like. Scott listened to Oasis and Frank Sinatra, that was it. Oasis was played every day of the week, along with videos of them being on tour. EVERY DAY OF THE WEEK FOR ELEVEN YEARS!

I had started to question whether he was a touch Asperger's. It would explain his difficulty in trying to live with day-to-day life. Along with this obsessive behaviour. I was living with his addiction to alcohol and steroids, drug use and Bipolar behaviour.

At this time, he had never used the internet. I was studying and needed the internet for my online studies. At the time, I was doing a Martial Arts Conditioning course. I thought it would be good with my coaching at The Bulldog. The martial arts world has no governing body that stipulates that you should be qualified in anything. Anyone with no understanding of anatomy and fundamental coaching skills can set up their own martial arts school. Crazy, right?

I introduced him to using a computer and the internet. Every time I switched on the computer to do my studies, the screen was always locked into a porn site. Katie Price hardcore was a favourite. Because he didn't know what he was logging into, he would fuck up my computer. I didn't care that he was looking at porn. All men look at porn. I just didn't want my computer fucked up. Of course, he didn't care and would fuck my computer anyway.

He had given up working as a care worker at that point and was now working full time as a nightclub bouncer at a club called the K Bar, which of course suited his drinking. The club was only ten minutes from our flat. It was within walking distance but he always took my car. I mean, it was literally ten minutes' walk down the road. But the lazy fuck that he was took my car. One night, when he brought it back, someone outside the club had kicked the driver's side window in and booted the driver's side mirror off. He said it was like that when he came out of the club after working. There was no offer to get it fixed. He, of course, didn't pay for it.

I went around trying to find out how to replace the window and get a new mirror. I ended up getting a salvaged one and fixing it myself.

One of his buddies that worked with him at the club told me that he had asked for a sip of his Red Bull. Scott handed it over. His friend took a sip and then spat it out because it was neat vodka. Again, I did not realise the extent of the drinking and how he was hiding it.

At this time, while Scott worked at the K Bar, every Saturday morning was spent puking his guts up. His excuse was that he stopped at Bunnies on the way home and got a crazy burger, blaming the bad food. Of course, I believed him. Why wouldn't I?

Same with the window of my car. Why wouldn't I believe the story he told me? I would never know the truth, of course. Just get on with things and keep living every day as it came.

We never had any money, ever! The debt was out of control. Scott was being sent credit cards left, right and centre. It was crazy. I would find one and say, 'What the fuck are you doing with that?'

'They sent it to me.'

Fifteen hundred pounds here, two thousand, five hundred pounds there. Halifax sent him a card for three and a half thousand pounds' credit limit! There was no way he had the funds to pay that back. But when you have companies sending you free money, of course you go out and spend it.

Scott did not have a clue about money. Scott thought twenty pounds would buy you a week's food shopping. He did know how to spend it though, without any thought as to how we were paying bills, rent, car, etc..

It's so weird when I think about it now. I could have walked away at any time in the beginning or anytime through the eleven years I gave him. I still try to figure out now what happened to me. Where did I go?

I had to go back on the door along with trying to keep my coaching and personal training business afloat. We needed money, so I had to do more work.

Scott asked if I wanted to do a couple of nights at the K bar. I said, 'Sure.' My knee felt strong enough to stand on for a length of time, and Scott was there if there was any trouble. He was good for that. For all the shit he put me through behind closed doors, I always knew that he wouldn't let anyone hurt me, that was certain. I knew I had a good team to work with, just in case it kicked off and I had the potential of being hurt.

When you arrive at the club you are given a position to stand in. This club had three different floors. I was down in the basement by the dance floor. Off I went, found my position and started to survey who was coming in. I had to keep my eyes peeled for dickheads who want to fight and drug dealers. I had a bit of local fame because of the fighting. That meant I would get random people coming up to me talking about the fighting, along with knob-jockeys who thought it was funny to wave their fists in my face and ask to see my skills!

Smiling and pretending to laugh I would try to brush them off. See them on their way in the hopes that they would not come back. This one guy, this particular night, kept coming back. I cannot move. I was working so I have to stay in my position. This dude can do what he likes. Go anywhere he wants. But decided that he was going to get pissed out of his face and kept coming back time after time after time, waving his fists in my face asking to see my skills. After three hours of this, I'd had enough. I mean what does he want me to do? Punch him full on in the face? Kick him in the legs? Knee him in the body? I could do a multitude of things to him that could have really hurt him. So, this is what I decided. I punched him in the stomach! Not too hard, but hard enough for him to fuck off and leave me the fuck alone. He stood there in front of me for at least two minutes, holding on to his stomach and did not say a word. He then fucked off. I didn't see him again for the rest of the night. GOOD!

Not long after that incident, a fellow doorman came over and told me to go upstairs. You would get relieved from your position as an inside doorperson just to have a change of scenery and essentially try and keep you fresh and not bored from being in the one position all night. As I was just about to get into my next position, another dude decided he was going to do the same thing. Started waving his fists in my face, asking to see my skills. I was like, nope, no way am I going to have this dude for the rest of the night testing me. So, I just gave him a teeny weeny knuckle cuff to the chin. He stood there startled, holding on to his chin! I said to him, 'You wanted to see my skills?' He left me alone after that as well.

What did they expect when they ask a full contact fighter to see their skills? What did they think I was going to do, tickle them? Idiots!

Scott was meant to pick me up from coaching one evening. As always, I stood out on the street waiting for him to turn up. I slowly start to fume because it has now been thirty minutes. I saw my car coming down the road with the front of the bumper missing.

He apologised and said, 'You are not going to believe what has just happened!'

He was leaving his mum's to come and pick me up. He was sat at a junction, waiting to pull out. This car came careening down the road and smashed into my car, then just took off. Scott had seen that the guy in the car was on his phone. This was around the time that the government had just brought in the law about being on your phone while driving your car.

Scott took off after the car and cut him down. I think he might have even gotten him to mount the pavement. Scott got out of my car and stood outside the driver's side of the car. Scott is a foreboding character, especially when he's angry. I would not want him outside my car window furiously asking me to get out of my car! Scott told me that he was just about to start smashing in the driver's side window. The man sat in the car was trying to tell Scott he was a police officer!

Scott managed to somehow get the policeman's phone off of him and his wallet. I'm not sure how he did that. He still had the possessions when he picked me up. We were now back at our flat. The policeman's phone rang and asked if he could come and pick up his wallet and phone.

He came into our flat very sheepishly, then apologized profusely. He took one look at my medals and the World Champion belt that was in the front room and assumed that they were Scott's. He said that he wouldn't stand a chance against Scott!

Scott laughed and said, 'They are not mine. They belong to her.' He pointed at me.

You know for a fact he was going, 'Oh shit, what have I walked into?'

If Scott had not chased the policeman down. I would never have had my car fixed. It would have been a hit and run. I think he thought we would be out for blood. Go to the papers, rinse him and the police force for being negligent. I am not that person. I told him to just fix my car. I didn't care about the rest.

Fortunately for me, my paperwork was always up to date. We had two police officers turn up to our flat to check our paperwork. I knew for a fact they were looking for a way out. Never mind that the other police officer had been in an unmarked car on his phone, smashed into my car and drove off! One rule for them, another rule for everyone else!

I Say I Do

Mine and Scott's intimacy had really started to break down. It was a weird time. I didn't know what was happening to me. I was struggling with his behaviour. I was depressed. I didn't know how to get out of the situation I was in. I didn't realise I was being manipulated. I actually went to the doctor because I thought there was something wrong with my vagina. The doctor referred me to the hospital. I saw a lady doctor that examined me. She told me she could not find anything wrong. She proceeded to ask me if I still loved my partner? That question threw me a bit. I felt embarrassed. I know now I wasn't being honest with myself. I honestly thought there was something wrong with me. With my clitoris, it didn't feel the same when he was kissing me and I should feel turned on. I blamed myself, when really it was my body saying no. He, of course, would ask what was happening. I didn't know how to explain it. The more it felt like that, the more I felt like my vagina was broken. I did think that maybe I had damaged it from being kneed and kicked there too many times. Or from all my bike riding. You do hear about guys damaging their undercarriage from too much cycling. This, of course meant lots of arguing because he wanted sex and I just didn't feel right or want to do it with him.

Scott wasn't very clean, either. Getting him to wash was a bit of a battle. There was one time, when we were getting down to sexy time, that, let's say, we had an issue with smegma. It just turned my stomach. I thought, 'No fucking way am I going near that!'

We had another massive row, probably over sex. I wanted out. I wanted to leave. But he would start to cry and beg me not to leave him. I would feel sorry for him. He would then tell me he was going to kill himself, which I believed. I did not understand manipulative behaviour back then. The 'kill yourself' stroke is a master move in keeping you tied to a relationship with someone. It played on my conscience. I could not have that on my shoulders. I did not want to be responsible for someone killing themselves. So, I stayed.

Our wedding was looming. My friend Debs said to me one day, 'Are you sure you want to do this?'

Debs had two black leather couches that sat opposite each other. I sat on one and Debs on the other. I said, 'Well why not? No one else has asked me to marry them.'

Apart from Rafael six years before.

On reflection now, I wasn't being honest with Debs. I hadn't told anyone about his behaviour and how he was. I'm not sure why. I also said, 'If it doesn't work out, I'll get a divorce!' Just like that! Really flippant, like it would be that easy just to walk away. I was kidding myself, trying to reassure my friend, who was looking out for me. Who wanted to know was I OK? Could I sort it out?

Thinking back to that now, I wonder: what the fuck was I doing?

No one was invited to the wedding. I didn't want anyone to come. I didn't want any fuss. Deep down inside, I did not want to do it. But I didn't know how to get out of it.

Off we went to Cyprus to get married. I did not wear white. I had bought an oriental dress in lilac and silver, with silver heeled sandals. It looked cool.

We had no money!

Stupidly, I applied for a loan before we left. I wanted to make sure we would have enough while we were out there. He certainly wasn't going to do it. He never planned anything. He never thought about the what ifs. I was being bumbled along on the crest of a wave of what he wanted to do.

People always alluded to the fact that I was a strong woman. I mean, I was a world champion Thai boxer. Unfortunately for me, I have a vulnerability that is deep inside because of my childhood. A narcissist that is looking for a human to control and break down will hone in on their weaknesses and take full advantage of them. I had lost my voice in this situation because of the manipulation. It was a drip, drip, drip of working away at my self-esteem. Before you know it, you are in a relationship with this person and there is no getting out of it.

The flight was super early in the morning, around six or seven a.m. We needed to be at the airport two hours before. We couldn't figure out anyone to give us a lift, especially at that time in the morning. Getting on the coach was the only option. This meant travelling through the night and arriving at the airport around four in the morning. Doing a night ride on a coach with super upright seats is not fun. He slept. I didn't.

Being at the airport was uneventful. Flying out to Cyprus was uneventful. Other than my 'What the fuck are you doing?' thoughts. Arriving in the sun with warmth on your skin was glorious.

That feeling you get when you step off the plane and feel that Mediterranean sun on your face is one of the best feelings in the world.

We arrived at our hotel room. The hotel room was not a honeymoon suite, but the hotel had put special touches in the room to congratulate us on getting married. A big bowl of fruit, flowers, and a note saying 'With compliments of the hotel, please come and book your meal to celebrate your marriage.' I just assumed that meant it was free!

If you say 'with compliments,' surely that means a meal on the house?

We had three days before the actual day. We decided to chill out, get some sun rays by the pool and get in touch with our marriage rep, who was organising everything for us.

The marriage rep was super cool. She thought that we were both refreshing to be with because we were not demanding.

She'd asked if we wanted pictures. We were not bothered. She then asked if we wanted a video. We were not bothered. She then asked if I wanted make-up, flowers, etc.

I said, 'No, I'm not bothered about that. I'll do my own make-up.'

I never wore that much anyway. She then asked about my dress.

I said, 'It's an oriental dress.'

She replied, 'How cool. You guys are so cool.'

The truth of the matter was, we could not pay for any of that. We had enough to be in the hotel for two weeks. We certainly didn't have enough to pay for extras. Scott had not planned for anything.

Would I have liked the extras? Of course. I would have liked to have wanted to be there. I would have liked to invite people. I would have liked a day of pampering for me and feel special. But there you go. Hindsight is a beautiful thing.

Scott did call his mum. Scott's mum was Scott's enabler. She did not know how to say no to him. If he ballsed up, she was always there to bail him out.

'We need five hundred pounds for pics and video.'

Scott's mum gave him five hundred pounds for the pics and video. It was embarrassing.

I have always stood on my own. I find it very difficult asking for anything, because there has never been anyone there to ask! Scott on the other hand had bank of Mum.

The day before our wedding day, we were in the hotel room. Scott wanted to go down to the pool. He was going to wear my flip flops. I said, 'NO!'

He of course, did not like that. He replied, 'What do you mean, "No"?'

'NO! You'll break them, and then what do I wear?'

His feet were size 11.

My feet were size 7.

The fact that I had said "No" incensed him. We had the biggest row. I sat out on the balcony and thought again, 'What the fuck am I doing? I'm stuck here. I'm about to marry this fucking idiot, and we have just had the biggest argument over flip flops.'

It wasn't about the flip flops. It was about me saying "No" to him.

Scott did not wear my flip flops. I bought him a pair, and they took all the skin off the top of his foot from the rubbing of the plastic. We were walking off the beach one day and he was ahead of me, trying to scrape the flip flops up the road with his feet. He could barely walk in them. I was laughing so hard on the inside. I thought to myself, 'You fucking idiot. Look at you now. You can't even walk in them and it has taken all your skin off! GOOD!' That was the end of the flip flops. He did not wear them for the rest of the trip.

The following day was the wedding day. I went down to the reception to arrange our complimentary meal with the restaurant manager. It turned out, as he stated, 'Nothing is free!' Oh my god! He was so rude to me. His whole attitude towards me was contemptuous. 'What do you mean, free meal?' I showed him the note left in the room. He dismissed it with disgust. He said, 'It will cost you €80.'

The whole situation had thrown me. I was dealing with this situation on my own. Scott was sat down in the foyer of the hotel.

Which was just as well, because he had a temper on him. There was no middle ground with Scott. Had he been there trying to sort this and thought that the manager was trying to have one over on us, he, without a doubt, would have knocked him out.

The manager then wanted to know about champagne when we returned. I said 'No, thank you.'

His reply was again with disgust. 'What do you mean no?'

I said, 'No, thank you, we do not drink.'

His response was to huff and shrug his shoulders like he did not understand that. He then asked about the cake. I said, 'No, thank you.'

I mean, what were we going to do with the cake? He then proceeded to ask about family. I replied, 'There is no one.'

Well, that just about finished him off. He started talking to himself in his own language. Looked at me like I was a piece of shit and then reiterated the fact that the meal was not under any circumstances free, and that it would cost me €80.

I walked away, and said to Scott, 'We are going to the room. I'm phoning the rep.'

I re-told the whole situation. I was so angry. 'Who the fuck does he think he is?'

I told the rep, 'You need to deal with this and get back to me with an outcome.'

Not long after I had put the phone down to the rep, I had a call from reception to come to see the manager. He approached me, with his tail between his legs. He didn't apologise, but offered the meal with compliments of the hotel. As we were not having a wedding cake or champagne, we could have the meal instead. I behaved courteously, and returned to the room to get myself ready to get married!

The marriage was in the town hall of Paphos, Cyprus. We were both made to sit outside and wait to be called into the office, where the ceremony was to be held.

It was all very clinical and sterile. It was like I was outside the headmasters' room, waiting to be told off.

The marriage rep was going to be one of our witnesses. She had also roped someone in from the town hall who was a worker to be our second witness.

Scott was called in first. I was then to follow five minutes later, by myself.

I've been thinking about why I did not want anyone there at the wedding. Obviously, I really didn't want to do it. But also, I have no family. Do you know what it is like to think that no one from your side of the family is going to even be bothered to be there? I hate it. It upsets me. Another reminder that you are all on your own, with no one to bother about you.

My dress looked beautiful, and my stiletto sandals looked great when I was standing still, but, for my life, I could not walk in them. A transvestite can walk better in heels than I can. I walked into that room like I'd shit myself.

Anyway, I was in the registry room and now shit was getting real! I was stood there like a deer caught in headlights. He was reading his part of the vows. I was laughing uncontrollably, but not in a happy, joyful way; it was hysterical. What the fuck was I doing? The registrar looked at me and said, 'Now you no laugh!'

I thought, 'Oh my god, how the fuck do I get out of this now?' The registrar started reading me my vows and before I knew it, I said, 'I DO!'

I signed the piece of paper. We were now fucking married! I had to try and make this work.

Mrs Mahoney

We arrived back at the hotel. There were staff and hotel guests waiting for us as we walked in through the foyer, clapping and celebrating our wedding day. It was so embarrassing. If my memory serves me right, Scott went straight up to the room and took a nap.

In the evening, we went and had our meal in the restaurant, with compliments! It was such a joke. They had set our table up outside of the main restaurant away from the guests of the hotel. A lone table, all on its own, set up on the patio with a posh candle on it! We were to help ourselves to the buffet for our starter. The restaurant staff kindly let us order our meal instead of collecting it from the buffet. Whoopy Doo! That was the only difference. This was 2003. €80 for a meal for two was quite a lot of money for what they were offering. I would not have paid €80 for that!

Although, thinking about it, the restaurant manager probably skimped on giving the full experience because we were not paying for it.

Wedding night. No passion. No sex. No intimacy.

That was down to me. I just couldn't find it in myself to do it. The internal conversation in my mind was, 'I want out of this whole situation.' On the outside, I was playing a role of not being responsible for his death.

The only thing I could hold on to was not fully giving myself over. I wasn't turned on. I did not want to have sex with him. I just couldn't do it. I now know in the end that was my saving grace in the whole time we were together. If I had given that up as well, I would have been a broken human being. Having sex for sex's sake is just not for me. I have to have some kind of emotional attachment. Otherwise, each time you have sex a little bit of your soul is taken away from you.

To be honest, I thought my vagina was broken as well.

The loan that I had applied for before we left had arrived. I had £2000 in my account. We had just been laying around the hotel or going to the beach. We decided that we needed to go and see some sights.

Off we went to the local tourist tours shop and saw straight away that they were doing trips to Egypt for the day. You could either go by boat over-night, or fly, which only took an hour. We decided we would fly. Of course, I paid for this out of the loan. £650 for the day trip to Egypt.

The day started at five a.m., and the flight was at seven a.m. The whole plane was full of tourists on the same trip. We had a rep for the day that was teaching us words in Arabic to say 'NO' and 'Go Away!'

They prepared us for the barrage of scammers and beggars that were going to be around the pyramids and markets.

The itinerary for the day: first stop, a famous mosque. I can't remember the name. But I remember it was big and gold, and that's about it. Next stop, the pyramids. When we were driving from the airport to Cairo you could see the pyramids as a back-drop to the city. It's really surreal, because there they are! One minute they are in a book and the next you are in a coach seeing them as a sky-line.

We had forty-five minutes to see them. If you wanted to get inside you had to be quick. Apparently, the tunnel is very small

31

leading into the pyramid. I thought, 'I don't think that is a good idea!' Especially as I was in a place where I was not coping well with my anxiety. Having a panic attack in a small tunnel surrounded with people was not the way forwards

Leading up to the pyramids, the reps told us not to accept anything from the blaggers that would try and get money out of the tourists there. You were to ignore them and take nothing.

Scott said, 'I've got to take a pee, I'll meet you out there.'

Off I went towards the pyramids. I was having this internal conversation with myself. 'I'm here. There they are, but I feel nothing.' I mean don't get me wrong, the pyramids are a wonder. But I was expecting to feel something, to be moved spiritually or something. Nothing. Emptiness. Dirty. Shady. Feeling super unsafe.

As I stood there, I made eye contact with one of the blaggers, who made a bee-line for me. Before I knew it, I had a head scarf thingy on, a postcard and replica pyramids. I had everything the reps told me not to take in my hands.

All of a sudden, Scott arrived. 'Did you listen to nothing?'

He then ended up with a scarf thingy on his head, but he did manage to get rid of them without having to give them money.

I said to him, 'They were being so friendly. I didn't want to be a complete asshole to them.'

We decided to get a bit closer to the main pyramid. I can't remember the name of the pyramid we were in front of. Me and Scott were getting pictures of each other standing on the fallen pyramid bricks. There was some sort of security officer or policeman standing right where we were taking pictures. He offered to take the picture of both of us. On return of the camera, he asked for money. Scott and I both refused. I think it held us in good stead that Scott was eighteen stone of muscle and I looked like I could handle myself as well. The security guy didn't pursue it. We walked away back to our coach.

As we were walking back, there was this man that was in our group. He must have been in his late eighties or early nineties. Nobody was looking out for him. Or even looking after him. We both saw him being haggled onto a camel by one of the blaggers. God knows where they were going to take him. He certainly would not have made it back in time for the next part of the coach tour. Scott went over and managed to pull him away. The Egyptian blaggers started to size Scott up. One of them said, 'Oh yeah, big man? What you got!'

'Right,' I thought, 'here we go. Try and keep him calm. Pull him away from the situation so that he doesn't feel like he needs to see it through and stand up for himself.'

I managed to get him and the old man back on the coach. We were then on to our next destination, the Sphinx. That was pretty cool. Although, again we were hassled by really young kids who were trying to sell postcards. Their selling pitch was, 'Cheaper than Asda, cheaper than Tesco.' How did they know about those supermarkets and use that as their selling pitch?

The hassling was full on. You were not to give over your camera, because if you did, you were not getting that back without handing over a sizable amount of money.

Off we went after the Sphinx to a papyrus shop. I had a book-mark made in Egyptian hieroglyphs that spelled my name. It was cool learning about the different characters and how it spelled out your name.

As we were being driven around in our coach, the local people were not best pleased to see us. There was a lot of animosity towards us. I then realised we had armed guards at either end of our coach taking us from place to place on our day trip. So weird. These people put us all in the same basket, much the same as the people in Britain that think that all Muslims are terrorists, or all people of colour are drug dealers and that everyone that grows up on a council estate is just the scum of the earth.

But what do they know? From my observation the poverty in Cairo far outstrips anything we have here. The lower classes of society living in unfinished buildings, with no windows or roofs. Buildings with the metal struts sticking out the top. They are living in these buildings so that they do not have to pay tax. The surrounding areas they are living in look like a bomb site. No green, just big massive spaces of unfinished building work and rubble.

From what I understand there are a certain number of families in Egypt that hold all the wealth. They intermarry within those families so that the wealth is not lost outside of those families. The rich stay rich and the poor stay poor.

Why are some human beings so inherently greedy and selfish? Why wouldn't you want to help everyone lead a comfortable life. Not excessive, but a nice home, and a good education. Learn to give back.

Greed. I hate greed!

What those Egyptians don't realise is that the lower working class in Britain have their own fight on their hands to try and survive. The lower classes are still fighting to get out of the council estates.

I know that I am a better human being having fought my way out of the lowest class in society in Britain. I know what it is to have to fight for my worth in this country. I also have compassion and understanding for those same people that are trying to do the same to survive. This is just my opinion. I feel the elite in this country are so out of touch with what is truly going on in the lower classes. I mean good for them, going to their elite schools like Eton and having the opportunity to get schooled at the best of the best. Such as Oxford and Cambridge, but what does that really show them. Nothing! Yes, they have the education but are so out of touch with the majority of the rest of the country that is essentially holding it all together. Because lets have it right, the companies that are earning the billions of pounds are not giving back to our system. It's the working class that are paying back.

I think they should all spend two to three years living as the lower classes do. Minimum wage. Living on an estate. Trying to survive. Just like the rest of us have to. Get a little taste of what it is like for the rest of society, so that they can make better and more informed decisions on how to run the country when they go back to mixing with their Eton buddies.

Anyway, I went off a bit of a tangent there. Back to the trip.

After the papyrus shop, we went to lunch at a five-star hotel. The food was amazing. This was followed by a trip down the Nile on a steamboat. The day was then finished off with the coach tour to the markets in the evening. I was not one bit fussed about getting off the coach. I did not feel safe in Egypt. The day for me was done. I wanted to go home or at least back to the hotel in Cyprus.

It was a bit of an anti-climax really. I went, I saw, I never want to go back. I'm just glad we did it as a day trip.

The rest of the stay in Cyprus was uneventful. I don't remember us falling out again. We were now just existing with each other. He had gotten me to sign on the dotted line which meant I had to stay. I was in a place where I was figuring out how I was going to make it work.

When we arrived at the airport to fly back to England, I was really stressed. I couldn't figure out why. I just didn't want to get on the flight. I didn't share that with Scott. I was internalising it. Something wasn't right. But I just put it down to my panic attacks and anxiety.

My panic attacks had surfaced while I was living in California when I was around twenty-four. They came from nowhere! One minute I was driving my car and going places on my own. All of a sudden I was not able to get into my car and travel without feeling like an attack was going to come on. The attacks did subside for a while on my return to the U.K. But an attack cropped up when I was fighting for my Commonwealth title. I put that down to the amount of stress I was under trying to make weight. They disappeared for a little while to then really take hold of me when my relationship started with Scott. I can't explain them. I don't feel like I am going to die. It is a chemical response in my body. It is like a turbo force of unexplained fear, where all my energy leaves my body.

We boarded the plane and settled down. The flight attendants brought round the food. I was starving. I ate everything on my tray and anything that Scott had left, I gobbled down too.

It was probably an hour into the flight that we started to hit some turbulence. Nothing crazy. I've been through turbulence before so I thought it would be over in no time.

The turbulence started up again but this time it was much worse. Before you knew it, the flight attendants were buckled into their seats and the TV's were switched to silence. The whole plane was silent. Everyone had stopped talking. The plane was shaking like crazy.

We were now fifteen minutes into this situation and there was no let up. I kept looking at Scott and reiterating that I didn't like it. He said, 'At least we'll be together if we die!'

I didn't want to die. My stomach was going topsy turvy with the food as well. It was super full and being shaken up by a massive metal tube that was now trying to flip over. All of a sudden the plane felt like it wanted to flip from the right side.

Around twenty minutes in, the captain came over the speaker. He was trying to reassure us that he was doing everything he could to get us out of a storm we were flying through. The plane was being hit by one hundred and seventy mile an hour winds on the right side. That's why it felt like it wanted to go over.

Gripping the arm handles like my life depended on it, I prayed we got through this without plummeting towards the earth and dying. It was so scary.

Forty minutes had passed. It felt like five hours. We were out the other side. That day was not the day for Janine to die, thank goodness. It was an added bonus as well that I managed to keep my food down!

Making It Work

We did have a discussion on surnames. I didn't want to change my name. I am Janine Davis. That is who I am. Why did I have to change my name? We did discuss Janine Davis - Mahoney. Scott said, 'No. No hyphens.'

When I think about that now, I think 'Who is he to decide? It's my name. I'll decide what I am going to be called. I am not five years old asking permission from a parent.'

Of course, I didn't challenge it. Where had I gone? It still baffles me. My voice. My opinion. Who was I?

He did not want to be called Scott Davis. So, reluctantly, I became Janine Mahoney. It took me ages to change everything over. I did not want to do it.

I took on the role of wife. I am always better when I am looking after people. I am not used to anyone looking after me. I'm not sure I know how to be looked after. It doesn't mean that I don't want that. I just don't want to have to ask for it. Surely if a person loves you they should just want to do it.

I got my head down. If I wasn't paying the bills and keeping a roof over our head, then no one was going to do it. If I stepped out of that position, Scott certainly wasn't going to do it. If I left him to sort it, we would have ended up being homeless.

There were days that I would lay in our bed thinking of ways of getting out of the marriage. I would think, 'OK, give it a year. I can't do it straight away'. Why couldn't I do it straight away? What was I thinking! But then I would think, 'Where am I going to go? I've got no money. Everything I earn is poured into keeping both of us afloat.'

The bills were mounting up like you wouldn't believe. The credit card bills were out of control. Scott just didn't give a monkey's. I would spend whole mornings trying to sort payment arrangements out for both of us.

What I didn't realise was that I was slipping slowly into depression and my panic attacks were out of control. No one knew what was going on because I didn't tell anyone. Every time I stepped outside the door for work it was show time. My security was my phone. If I started to weird out or feel like an attack was coming on, I would call someone. I couldn't drive long journeys without the fear engulfing me. Even going to the gym was starting to become an issue if I was having a bad day.

Scott was now hanging out at a local pub called the Litten Tree. I was spending more and more time at home, shutting myself away from friends.

One night he had taken my car. I stayed home to get some peace by myself. I had taken myself off to bed fairly early. I could hear *tap tap tap* on the window. I wasn't sure of the time. We were in the bottom floor flat. I opened the window. It was Scott. I barked at him, 'Where are your keys?' I looked at my phone. It was three a.m.!

His response: 'They are in the car.'

'Go and fucking get them then.'

In his pissed-up state he said, 'It's not here.' I closed the window and reluctantly went and opened the front door.

At this point we were still sharing the same bed. Although the bed was not big enough for the both of us. It was a queen size. Him being eighteen stone and me not small at all – five foot eight and twelve stone – it was never a restful sleep. I am never good at being woken up in the middle of the night. We quite regularly had rows about him coming to bed and waking me up. I liked to go to bed at ten p.m., Scott liked to go to bed at three a.m. I have a full day of physical activity. He would lay in bed until maybe midday, until he decided to get up and go to work. I would be woken up at three a.m. and not be able to get back to sleep. It was like a baby elephant getting into bed next to me. He never once thought about me or how maybe, just maybe, waking me up at three a.m. most nights would affect my day. I think that may have been the root cause of putting his fist through the door.

Anyway, the following day Scott was hung over and is just lying around the flat. I was taking care of admin as per usual. I kept asking, 'When are you getting my car?'

'In a bit.'

This went on for hours, until finally he phoned his friend, who came and collected him around four p.m. After about an hour of waiting for him to return with my car, I phoned him. 'You've lost it, haven't you?'

'I've looked everywhere, I can't find it!'

I threw the phone into the couch. I mean, what the actual fuck? That mother-fucker has lost my car. What the fuck am I going to do about getting around for work? I had Thai boxing sessions to get to where I had to take kit, three big duffel bags full of Thai pads and gloves. There was no way I was walking with it! We needed money and I needed to keep working!

That mother-fucker!

He returned to the flat where he then started to confess about the evening before and how he had come to lose my car.

It turns out he was in The Litten Tree getting shit-faced. One of his mates turned up with his brother and explained that they were going to go and get some money that was owed to their dead dad. They figured that the guy needed to pay up and that he was not going to get away with it.

Scott, in his infinite wisdom, thought it was a good idea to drop them off. He drove them both to the guy's house. They were both wearing balaclavas and carrying a knife each. This would have been probably two in the morning. He dropped them and decided to drive home.

The two brothers decided to kidnap this guy and escort him to cash machines to get the money that was owed to their dead dad, using the knives to hold him to ransom.

Scott, while driving home, was fucking about with the radio when a police car drove past. He was clearly driving erratically because the police decided to turn around and follow him. Scott shat himself and took off down the road to escape. He turned the car round. The police car and Scott pass themselves. Scott took off. He explained that he took a left, another left and another left, then dumped the car and took off running. He then explains that he hid behind a bush to see the police car drive past looking at 'my car' without him in it. The police did not stop and missed their opportunity to grab him. He then decided to walk home. Hence waking me up by knocking on the bedroom window at three a.m.!

Scott thinks CID had got the car and was looking for fingerprints. We then found out that the brothers had armed response come to their house while they were sleeping for the bullshit they had pulled, for kidnapping the guy with a knife and extorting money out of him.

Scott's a fucking idiot!

I reported the car stolen. Yes, it was a pain in the ass, but I was hoping to get a pay-out and a new car. No such hope. A friend of mine phoned me a week later and said she had found it. It was on a road on the opposite side of the main road where Scott had been looking. Such a twat, and a lazy twat at that. I phoned the insurance company and said it had been found so not to worry. I went and picked it up.

Why didn't I leave then?

I'll keep repeating this. Why didn't I leave? Where had all my strength gone? Unfortunately, when you grow up in dysfunction, you do not know right from wrong. I just thought it was the norm. This was just how life was going to be. We were married. I was trying to make it work.

Some of Scott's friends were doormen at The Litten Tree and had asked him to cover some nights. They were also looking for a female door person. I ended up working at The Litten Tree as well. Thinking about it, I don't think me and Scott ever worked together there on the same night. Which seems weird actually. He was probably doing stuff that he didn't want me to see elsewhere.

One night, after returning from work at two a.m., I needed to be in bed and asleep quick smart. I had a client at eight a.m. for Thai boxing. As I was trying to fall asleep, there was this bass beat vibrating through the whole building.

Our block of flats was mostly occupied by old people, eighty-plus, along with me and Scott. Sort of quietly living, apart from the loud altercations! There was a flat two floors up that the agents of the flat had, for some reason, moved in a couple of twenty-year-old boys. This block was not for them. They had people coming and going day and night. Up and down the stairwell, up and down in the lift, all hours of the night. The music was always pumping out of the flat and that bass beat late at night goes right through you.

There was no way I was getting any sleep with that music pumping through the flats. I sat upright and said, 'Fuck this, I'm going up.'

Scott got up as well and we both went up.

Scott only had on his joggers. When he had no top on, he looked massive. Not someone you would want to get into a ruck with. Especially twenty-year-old, skinny, white boys!

We went up in the lift to the flat. I rang the doorbell and stood right in front of the peephole. Scott stood to the side so that he could not be seen. I was in my pyjamas. I looked unassuming. As soon as the door opened, Scott shoved the idiot out of the way and walked through the flat with me in tow. The dude on the door didn't have a clue what the fuck was happening.

Scott walked straight into the living room where they were all sitting. Probably around six to seven people all sat around talking shit and drinking. I could see drug paraphernalia on the table in the middle of the room. There was a dude at the stereo. They all looked up, surprised and scared at the fact there was an eighteen stone, muscle on muscle, naked man in their living room. Scott told them, 'Turn your fucking music down!'

I stood behind him, ready to go if I needed to. One of the young men sat in the room very quickly said, in a very squeaky voice, 'Yeah mate, no problem.'

We turned, left the flat and went back to our flat. Silence was golden.

I had been asked to do an interview for a martial arts magazine, which was pretty exciting. I was a world champion. I was being promoted as a world champion. It was so cool.

'Janine Davis, World Champion.'

I had to do some demonstrations. I was nervous about it because my knee was still really unstable. I was waiting for my first operation appointment. I was training on it, but not really kicking. I was trying to get some muscle hypertrophy in my right leg so that the atrophy in my knee after the operation would not be so rapid, and my recovery would be faster.

I remember asking Dave if I could put my knee sleeve on. I asked permission. Again, not thinking about myself. I didn't want to let anyone down. He said yes, it was OK.

A true female athlete is not in a full face of make-up and all the bullshit that comes with over-feminising ourselves to make sure that we are accepted. I am an advocate for what you see is what you get. Au naturel, take it or leave it. I am not doing anything else to present myself. That's how I did the article.

After the interview, I sauntered over to the martial arts shop and noticed a martial arts magazine from Australia sitting on the side. I opened it up and on the inside there was a two and a half page spread on me. The headline: 'Disgrace in the U.K.' What the actual fuck? This was about three months after the fight.

Why are Australians such bad losers when it comes to sport?

The whole article was about me. I didn't read all of it, but did read the final paragraph where they stated that they were pleased to hear that I had ended up in hospital with a broken knee.

Is that good sportsmanship?

Did I kick up a fuss when she walked away with the Commonwealth title after I broke my wrist? NO! I took it on the chin and just accepted it.

It turns out that Louise O'Donnell had been calling Dave, telling him to send the title to her and that she was the winner of that fight. She and her team kicked up such a fuss that they went to the WPKL who had sanctioned the fight on the night with three judges that had been paid to sit around the ring and judge. The WPKL came back to Dave and said they had watched the video after three months and decided that they were going to overturn the decision.

Have you ever heard of anything so fucking ridiculous in your life? What was the point in having judges? You may as well have pulled three people out of the crowd with no experience whatsoever and gotten them to judge. I was so fucking angry.

Dave was meant to deal with it. Dave, I know, didn't deal with it. Dave is weak and doesn't like confrontation. Dave's a bit of a coward.

I have since found articles on the internet that have written horrible untruths about me, and that fucking stupid twat Louise O'Donnell thinks that she has the title. Well, fuck you! I kept the belt and I kept the title.

Getting My Knee Fixed

My appointment came through for my knee surgery. To be honest, I didn't really understand what they were going to do, or what the outcome was going to be.

Going for surgery is a strange journey. I know for myself that I questioned whether or not I was going to wake up from the operation. What happens if I wake up whilst they are drilling into my knee and I can't tell them?

I had had anaesthetic before when I was eleven. They had to reset my arm after that lovely individual that lived in my area growing up stamped on it. I knew that anaesthetic made me vomit violently.

You question things differently as you age. I certainly wasn't thinking about my mortality when I was eleven. I just didn't want them to set my arm when I was awake, no fucking way!

After sitting around for seven hours waiting for my knee surgery, I was getting myself worked up. A nurse came into the room I was sat waiting in, and asked me follow him.

It's so weird going into the operating theatre. You walk in and you are told to jump up onto the metal couch, a trolley bed with wheels. You are then asked a load more questions while you are laying on the top of this metal couch. You are not taking anything in because you think that you are never going to wake up again. They shove a needle in your hand. The first drug they give you is a muscle relaxant, Ooh, that feels so good. Your body goes really floppy. It reminds me of being high and floating around the clubs when I was a teenager. You are then told to start counting to ten. I don't even get past one. The next thing you know, you are being brought round by one of the nurses. You think that that is the first time you have been awake, but apparently you will have been awake before, chatting bollocks. Oh, to be a fly on the wall, listening to the nonsense that is coming out of your mouth when you are coming out of theatre.

Why does the consultant always come and speak to you when you are out of it? The consultant came and spoke to me, told me what he had done and gave me a little tub with my cartilage in it. The piece was massive!

Two rounds of toast and butter. A nice cup of green tea. If you can lift your leg up and down you are allowed to go. I could lift my leg up and down without any issue at all. I was good to go home.

They gave me crutches which I never used. They also gave me loads of painkillers that I never took. My pain threshold is good. I can manage my pain. I tried taking that Oramorph. It's liquid morphine they send you home with. Some of my buddies had spoken about how it made them feel amazing. I tried it. I didn't see what all the fuss was about. It did nothing for me. So I binned that. Just made me feel weird.

The day after surgery, Scott was helping me to the shop as I was still a little uneasy on my knee. We bumped into the young men that lived two floors above us, who would party all night, every night! One of the guys spoke to Scott and said, 'All right, yeah, we are just moving all our stuff out. We've found a place up the road.'

Scott very calmly replied, 'OK. See you around.'

We carried on to the shop with Scott holding on to my arm. As we walked off Scott told me those are the guys from upstairs.

47

I went and had a talk to them.

Prior to my surgery I bumped into one of the elderly ladies that lived in the block. We got chatting, and I asked her which flat she lived in. As it turned out, she was in the flat above ours. I said, 'Oh my goodness, how do you deal with noise?'

The elderly lady got very upset and kept repeating to me, 'They are not going to run me out of my home!'

My thoughts right there and then were 'Enough is enough!' I was going to do something about this. Me and Scott could just about deal with it. But, this elderly lady in her eighties was completely distraught about the whole situation. I wrote to the agency, and I tried to do it the right way. Scott decided he would do it his way. He waited for one of the young men to come back to the block while I was in hospital. He strung this lad up by his neck outside his flat and told him in no uncertain terms that they needed to go. He then said, 'My wife, she'll write to the agents. Do it the right way. Me, I am going to rip your fucking head off!' So that was that, they were gone and the peace was restored.

A couple of days of gingerly walking about and I was up and running. No pain, and I could put weight through my leg. I was good to go. After a week I was back in the gym working my rehab. The mission was to make my legs strong.

I settled into life with Scott and really it was just a day to day survival. I know that I managed to put on a show for work. But, really other than work I just cocooned myself at home. I sunk into quite a low depression. I did not see anyone, I did not talk to anyone. Nobody knew what was happening.

My dad appeared at some point in our first year of marriage. He decided on a visit to the U.K. We hadn't really spoken that much after he had spent his time moaning to me about the fact that he had to pay child support to 'his' child: my half-sister

Ashley. I just couldn't believe it. He had never paid a penny towards me and Leigh's up bringing. He was then moaning to me about authorities in the USA chasing him to pay. Such a dick. I had distanced myself from him, but hadn't at this point stopped talking to him.

It's so stupid. I wanted to show him where I was living. Get him to meet Scott. I wanted to show him my world title belt. He, of course, was not the one bit interested. He decided to meet me and Leigh in town at a pub with all his friends. It was so strange. Leigh turned up excited to see Dad. Dad surrounded himself with all his friends, and didn't really speak to me or Leigh. He certainly didn't want to know how I was. He then took off to the strip club.

I'm not interested in women's boobs, thanks. I did not want to go to the strip club. I took myself off home, let down again. Angry. I thought again, 'Fuck you and all your shit.'

My memory is vague. I'm sure I may have written him a letter. He thought I was angry about a fucking jewellery box that he had not brought over.

A fucking jewellery box! Are you fucking kidding? I mean, how stupid do you really have to be as a person? You have two children that you have spent no time with. All I want is time and interest in my life, and you think I was angry over a fucking jewellery box.

Such a selfish asshole.

My leg was getting stronger, so I was back in the fighting gym trying to kick. I was still missing that cruciate ligament in my knee to stabilise it. There was no way, if I wanted to get back to fighting, that I was going to be able to do it without getting it fixed.

I had gone to see the consultant for a check-up and had

decided to blag it a bit. To be honest, Scott did say you are going to have to lie. I am not a good liar. But if I wanted to get it fixed, I needed to tell them that my knee had started to collapse and that I was unable to get back to work.

In less than five minutes of seeing the consultant, he asked me how it was. I literally said it was no good. I didn't need to say anything else. He said, 'Fine we'll fix it.' So that was that. I was going to get my ACL rebuilt.

The mission now was to get the leg as strong as possible before the surgery so that my recovery would be swift, again!

ACL Rebuild

Cassandra had decided to come and visit. I was still in a very strange place. I don't know why, but I got Scott to go and collect her from the airport instead of myself. We were in so much debt and I was so consumed with working that I could not think about taking any time off. Also, my anxiety and panic attacks were so bad that there was no way I could drive on my own. I couldn't even sit on a coach for any amount of time without having an attack.

Seeing Cassandra was really cool, and we just hung out. True friends are friends that can spend any amount of time apart and pick up where they left off without there being any difference from before. We didn't really do too much, as I was working, but I did plan a night out at a club for us both to go to. I just wanted it to be me and Cassandra. Unfortunately, Scott had other ideas. I was so miffed. I just wanted some time alone, free of him to spend with my friend like old times. But no!

We were all waiting to get into the club in a queue and I could see that Scott was starting to behave oddly. His mate had turned up and they were both into taking GHB, 'liquid ecstasy' as they call it on the party scene. It is awful stuff. I never saw the fun in it. If you take too much, your heart stops and you die. Or you become completely incapacitated and shit yourself. Where is the fun in that?

Whatever his mate had given him, and whatever he had decided to take, Scott was starting to lose it before we had even gotten into the club.

I disassociated myself from him and let him get on with things with his mate. I tried to stay on the other side of the dance floor, away from him. But I could see him from the other side of the dance floor starting to really lose his shit. He was sweating profusely; at one point his mate was trying to pour a bottle of water down his throat. I could see Scott just standing there, caught in time with his gob wide open, with sweat pouring down him. It was at this point the security had started to close in. If we didn't get him out of the club then he was going to be asked to leave. I was so angry. I just wanted to have a good night with my friend.

We managed to get him down the stairs of the club and get him in a taxi. There was no way he was going to be able to walk it, even though our flat was literally a ten minute walk up the road from the club. We arrived at the flat, and less than five minutes later he passed out. Myself and his mate managed to carry him into the bedroom where I put him in the recovery position. He was still breathing; I just didn't want him to choke on his tongue or even on his own vomit.

It wasn't long before he came round and the vomiting started. That was how I spent the rest of the night. Keeping that twat alive.

When he did eventually come round and was able to walk, he spent his time peering at everyone in the living room through the crack of the door because of the state of paranoia he was in from the quantity of drugs he had taken – five to six ecstasy tabs and who knows how much GHB.

That was the last time I saw Cassandra in the flesh. I didn't talk to her about what was truly going on either. Not one person ever really asked me how I was. I must have been a really good actor. I did a really good job with getting my head down and just got on with things until I had my shit figured out.

I have actually failed to mention that the flat Scott had bought was at this point still filled with weed. That was an ongoing fucking issue. It was meant to have been cropped six months before but fuck knows what was going on. I was paying rent on the place we were living in, and now had to support the mortgage on the place that fucking monkey was trying to cultivate an income from by growing weed.

My second operation was now due. The hospital had sent me my appointment date. I thought 'Great, let's get this fixed.' I was up and on my feet in a week with no pain after the first operation. 'My recovery will be fine,' I thought 'I am good to go.'

The first operation had led me into a false sense of security. I thought that it would be pretty much the same procedure and I would be up and moving around in no time!

How wrong I was!

Any surgery is intense. You are not meant to be opened up and dug around in. The body doesn't like it. Never mind all the drugs they give you. The recovery from the drugs alone is enough. I was to be in hospital overnight on a twenty-four-hour bed rest. I was not allowed to move.

My particular ACL rebuild was a graft from my hamstring. My understanding is that they drill into your shin bone, screw the graft into that, pull it through your knee and tac it on to your thigh bone. It is truly amazing how they do it. But let me tell you, it is intense!

I had a nerve block put in at the top of my right thigh. I could not move any part of my right leg. I could not feel a thing. I tried to wiggle my toes for quite some hours after the surgery and it was not happening. When you had nurses coming round tickling the bottom of your feet and asking you if you could move your toes yet, and you said no, their response was always with a little surprise. They left you feeling like you were going to be paralysed down your right leg forever!

I laid there trying really hard to send messages down to my toes for ages, with nothing happening. It was scary.

I remember thinking, 'You know what? I haven't been to the toilet for ages.' I looked at the time; it was eight p.m. The last time I had been was at eight a.m. I thought that it was a good idea that I go. Because of the nerve blocker I could not feel my bladder. I pressed down on my lower belly and thought, 'Hmmm... I should definitely try to go!'

I pressed my buzzer for the nurse. She arrived like I was a total inconvenience to her. I said to her, 'I think I need the toilet.'

'You think or you know?'

'Well, I've not been since this morning and I can't feel anything. Do you think I should at least try to go?'

Off she went and returned with a bed pan. A fucking bed pan! I wasn't allowed to get out of bed. You boys, you can just whip out your penises and stick them in anything. The logistics of me, with my leg that is completely out of action and has to remain straight, trying to get on top of a cardboard bed pan in my bed to take a piss was not fun.

I managed to get myself on top of the shit piece of cardboard that I was meant to piss in, with the nurse stood there with her arms folded just looking at me. Not one piece of compassion in her at all. Fucking bitch! I sat there for a bit, nothing was happening. I looked at her and said, 'I can't do it with you stood there.'

She huffed and took off. Once she left, it started to come, and come and come. I thought I wasn't going to stop. I filled the whole thing up. I was now on my bed post-surgery, all my dignity taken away from me, left there to sit in my own piss because the bitch nurse couldn't be bothered to just wait outside of the curtain until I had finished. She decided to fuck off and just leave me there. I couldn't reach the buzzer, so I just sat there in tears waiting for her to come back. She pulled back the curtain to find me in a right state.

I mean, why go into a job where you are meant to care for people if you do not give a shit?

She cleaned me up as best as she could. I thought there was no way I was sitting on one of those again. But my body had other ideas.

The ward lights were turned off around nine thirty p.m. I laid there thinking I do not want to go to the toilet. But I always go to the toilet before I sleep. I laid there until one a.m. trying to forget about the fact that I did not need the toilet. I worked myself up into a right state crying, because I didn't want to wake anyone up on the ward. I did not want to sit on that piece of shit cardboard with all my dignity taken away either. I seemed to forget the fact that I was in hospital, and that the nurses were supposed to be taking care of me because I was not allowed to go home!

I gave in and rang the buzzer. The nurse appeared, arms folded. She was not best pleased with the fact that I had rung the buzzer. I seemed to get on with it second time round. Maybe because it hadn't been twelve hours since I had taken a piss! I didn't have so much piss coming out of me.

I laid back down and tried to go to sleep; this is when the pain started to kick in. The nerve block was starting to wear off. A different nurse came round at that point. She asked me if I was OK; she then said she would get me some pain killers and asked if I would like a cup of cocoa and some biscuits. Just that tiny bit

55

of compassion was so lovely. That's all it takes. I had my cocoa and biscuits with a cup of morphine, and finally drifted off to sleep.

At six a.m., all the lights in the ward were switched on. A nurse was on the ward, wakey-wakey people. I thought to myself, 'Who the fuck is this and what the fuck are they doing?' I put the sheet that was covering me over the top of my head and tucked it in the side so that I could block them out. Before I knew it there was a nurse by my side tapping me on the shoulder. Wakey-wakey, sleeping beauty. I begrudgingly pulled down the sheet and asked her what time the physio was coming round. She replied, 'Seven thirty a.m.'

'Great,' I said, 'because I am not sitting on one of those bloody bed pans again.' I was able to lift my leg up and down at that point. The nerve block had completely worn off now. My toes were wiggling freely, which was quite a relief. The reason for the early wake up was to take blood pressure. Six a.m. though!

Seven thirty a.m. came around and the physio appeared, a lovely older lady. I immediately asked her for crutches. She disappeared and came straight back with them. I set them up quick smart and took off across that ward to the toilets. I have never been so happy to shut the door to a toilet and take care of myself, without a moody cunty nurse standing over me.

The day was spent doing the necessary checks to make sure that I could go home. I messaged Scott and said I would be ready by four p.m. I was so bored. I was ready to go home. I just wanted to be around my stuff, with all my belongings. I also wanted to try and have a wash. I felt disgusting.

I was sitting on my bed in the ward ready to go at four p.m. Scott was always late. He was never on time for anything. Ten minutes I can forgive, but when I am waiting twenty minutes to half an hour, I start to get mad. No phone call. No explanation. There never was. I would think 'You selfish fuck. I'm in hospital. I've had quite an intensive operation on my knee. The least you can do is be on time to pick me up.'

When he eventually turned up, he was out of it. He was always taking pills to pick up his energy a bit. I can't remember what they were, maybe ephedrine. They were like speed. But instead of taking the pick me up pills he had taken some sleeping pills instead by mistake. He was feeling really tired and was struggling to keep himself awake. This motherfucker was going to drive me home!

I said, 'Just get me out of here!' I wasn't allowed to walk out. I had to be wheeled out in a wheelchair. I was so fucking cross. It took him another fifteen minutes to find the wheelchair.

Fortunately, we made it home in one piece. I slept the first night on the couch because I didn't want him touching my leg. That didn't work out so well. I was not very comfortable. In fact, even being in bed was not that great either.

It turns out I was not up and running around in a couple of days. Having your ACL reconstructed is nothing like getting your meniscus tidied up. I didn't sleep at all for at least two weeks post-surgery. The sensations and pain in my knee were weird, especially around where they screwed the pin into my shin bone.

I was on crutches for three months. My recovery from that surgery to get to the point where I could fight again took me two years.

Lifting Heavy Shit

Scott was now working as a night-time security driver. His job was to go around checking schools and other buildings in the middle of the night to ensure they were secure, and nobody bad was trying to break into them. From what I remember, most of these places were far out in the countryside of Dorset in the middle of nowhere. Scott had to swipe a security tag when he arrived and I know for a fact that he would swipe and run as fast as he could back to the car. These places at night were super creepy; big old Victorian buildings surrounded by big old oak trees and conifers. I remember this one time, he got caught short and needed to go to the toilet. Instead of going in the bushes like anyone else would have done, he had it in his head that if there were any creepy people around, lurking in the bushes, he would be grabbed. In his infinite wisdom he decided to take a dump in the middle of the school playing field. There, he had plenty of open space around him, so he couldn't be grabbed. I mean, it sounds like a good idea. But if you are going to take a dump in a school playing field, maybe don't use the paper with the security logo on it to wipe your arse and leave it with the poo! Idiot! Nothing ever came of that, but whoever found it would have known it was him!

That job was pretty horrible. Five nights on, two days off with no shift pattern to recover from the night work. He would start at five p.m. and get home around seven thirty a.m. You cannot sustain that for long. You will just get ill. Definitely not great with his bipolar...

At that time though, at least he was trying to work. We also had students living with us for extra money. In Bournemouth there are a lot of English speaking schools. These schools advertise for host families. Looking after the students was more work than I had anticipated. I had to do breakfast, lunch and dinner on the cheap. All of us living in the house had to creep around during the day in order not to wake Scott. It was a ridiculous situation, really. I was trying to keep my PT business running, whilst trying to rehab my knee. All of this on top of looking after the students and tip-toeing around the flat to keep him happy.

The student thing was doing my head in. The money we were getting for the hassle just wasn't worth the extra work for myself. So, I got shot of that.

Scott also stopped working the night shifts. It wasn't great for his depression. I can't remember what he did after that. I think he may have started at an autistic care house. I'm sure this was around the time I would come home to find all the autistic residents of the home in my flat.

Scott would take them all out and bring them to the flat whilst he made himself something to eat. In amongst his chaos and depression, there was compassion to look after these special-needs people. He was very good with them.

I was now well into the rehab of my knee. My anxiety and panic attacks were manageable. I just found ways to control my emotions should there be a trigger. I cannot pinpoint the triggers. Sometimes I would just feel the chemical response come on as I left the house. If I didn't have my phone that would definitely leave me feeling vulnerable to having at attack. There were certain routes I would not drive if I was feeling particularly

59

anxious. As I have said before, I would also keep my phone handy should I need to reach out to someone to snap myself out of the negative thoughts.

I was in the gym one day benching when a man approached me and said, 'I've seen you train before, you're quite strong. Would you like to be part of a female powerlifting team?'

'Amazing!' I thought, and replied, 'Yes, I would!'

He told me the place to go and meet him. I would start the following week. I thought, 'How cool is that!' It gave me something else to concentrate on whilst I was unable to fight.

Around this time, I was researching the next course to study. I already had my PT cert, a sports nutrition cert, and a martial arts conditioning cert. I was now looking at a nutritional medicine certification. It was super interesting. It basically covered treating the issue, as opposed to going to the doctors and taking medication to mask over the problem.

For instance, let's say you have high blood pressure. Ask the question: 'Why have I got high blood pressure?' Don't just take medication for high blood pressure. Once you ask the question as to why, maybe that issue can be treated and solved before you start chucking medication down your throat.

One story that sticks out in my mind from the course was a man that had gout and high blood pressure. He went to the doctors and they advised that he take medication that he would have to stay on for the rest of his life. We all know that taking medication may or may not come with problems further on down the line. You will start to have adverse effects associated to the drugs, leading to more problems. The man was unhappy with this solution and decided to get some tests done. The results showed a high level of lead that was sitting in his kidneys, which was causing the gout and therefore the high blood pressure. He went through a series of treatments to clear him of the lead in his body. All his symptoms went away without him needing medication. Now, you may ask, where the lead was coming from?

It was coming from the hair dye that he had been using for fifteen years! Products have changed considerably over time, but that does not mean that we are still not exposed to pollutants that can affect our bodies.

It was a fascinating course. Thanks to that course, I will always ask questions these days as to what may be happening to my body, should an issue arise. I will get to the root cause before I starting chucking medication down my body just because the doctors say so!

My training was slowly starting to pick back up at The Bulldog. Just boxing to start with, trying to build my confidence back up again. I tried to start moving around the ring with my knee. I had a training buddy, Liam, who was the boxing coach up in the gym. We had done a lot of training before the injury, so I had asked him if we could get back to it.

It was a weird time at The Bulldog. There was a lot of back stabbing going on and people not being honest. Dave was also being weird, though. I had started to distance myself from him. I had begun to realise that he really wasn't a genuine person at all. It was all about him and money!

Liam had agreed to start training with me. One morning we were boxing in the ring. I was super rusty and had lost a lot of my confidence in what I could do. I knew I wasn't hitting him hard. Or maybe I was? He decided he was going to let me have it. I took the first hit that knocked me back into the corner of the ring. It took me by complete surprise. I didn't know where it had come from. He landed another one, with real strong intent to hurt me. I then curled up in the corner, trying to protect my head. I could see his face through my gloves, and he had a real nasty expression on his face. He was really trying to put me on the floor. I had to tell him to stop. I had never done that before. I couldn't understand where it came from. Why did he want to do that to me? We had trained together so many times. I thought he was my friend.

That was the last time I trained with Liam. I certainly did not need to be put through that again.

I know I was a bit of an asshole back then. But when you are a fighter, there is a place you go to in your character to help you get through day after day of punishment you have to undergo.

Maybe there was jealousy over what I had achieved.

I did find out years later that he was dating one of the women in The Bulldog, who was a fellow instructor. She didn't care too much for me, and hated training with me. I know that there was a lot of chat going on in the shop behind my back about me. I think Liam saw it as his duty to make me pay. Especially when I was not in my strongest mindset.

I did contact him ten years after that incident and told him how it made me feel. He denied ever doing that to me. I know what happened as if it were yesterday. I could see and feel what was happening. He did apologise, which was cool. But it was really the end of what I had at The Bulldog before the world title fight. I had started to see the cracks in what was The Bulldog gym fight team. I approached Dave on numerous occasions and spoke to him about any issues that were happening. I asked to him to tell me if I was being an asshole. If he didn't tell me, how could I put it right? He always told me there was no problem. There was a problem; he just didn't have the balls to tell me.

Dave couldn't deal with confrontation.

Dave was a coward.

I never told Scott about that incident with Liam. I never told anyone about that incident with Liam.

Dave had gone on an American marketing course to upgrade the gym. He came back with a lot of new ideas on how HE was going to make money. I was teaching four classes a week and earning £25 a class. That was a pretty standard price twenty years ago. To be honest, that amount of money per class hasn't changed at all to this day.

Dave, with his new ideas, told all the instructors that we were now to go into town with a clipboard and were to stop the general public and ask them for their numbers. We were then to come back to the gym and call the numbers to get them to sign up to the new membership deals. Depending on how many students signed up, and what the gym was taking as far as money, the instructors would get paid ten per cent!

Bear in mind that by this point I had worked for Dave for four years, the first year of that for free. I had fought for him, never questioned not being paid for fights and had become a World Champion for the gym with a snapped knee.

I went from being paid £100 a week for four classes to £60 a month for the same amount of classes. I mean, what the fuck!

I would go into the shop and try and talk to him about it. Dave would say to me, 'It's nothing personal Davis, it's just business!' I'd look at him and think 'Fuck you. What am I doing?'

Around this time, I was offered a position to teach martial arts at another gym in Bournemouth. I didn't tell anyone about it. I kept it close to my chest, trying to figure out how and what I was going to do about it.

I refused to go into town to collect numbers. I wasn't going to do it. For £60 a month he could go fuck himself. I was in the shop again and was trying to have another conversation about the system. Dave was sat there like he was some kind of a gangster kingpin. I thought, 'Fuck you!' So, I told him I had been offered another gym. Dave's ears pricked up, and he got all bothered about how it was going to affect his gym. I said, 'My gym has got nothing to do with your gym.'

Dave then said, 'Are you going to keep it Bulldog?'

I said, 'NO! I'm doing it on my own.' Dave didn't like that.

'It's nothing personal Dave, it's just business!'

That was the end of our relationship. I had started to see the kind of person he really was.

This was the start of Machine Martial Arts. I was in charge of my own teaching and coaching, getting paid what I should be getting paid and not earning £60 a month for twelve classes. £5 a class, I mean come on! That is a fucking piss-take!

Alongside my personal training, I was now able to get back to doing a bit of door work as my knee was getting stronger. Me and Scott needed money! I was back working at The Litten Tree. It was known as a rough pub. It was one of the worst pubs I ever worked in for glassings and generally people being complete assholes. There was always trouble, but a couple of nights that stand out in my memory are as follows.

I was stood out on the front door like most Saturday nights that I worked at The Litten Tree. You are watching and observing the punters coming through the main doors. You are trying to keep out all the riff-raff. You have to be pretty astute to suss out the bad from the good. This one particular evening, a young man, probably early twenties, was walking up the steps to the door. I clocked him straight away. He looked like he had been fighting. I stopped him and said, 'Buddy, not tonight, you've been fighting.'

Generally, if they have been fighting, it means they are going to bring that aggression into your pub and you can just do without it.

He promised me that the bruising on his face was from last week. I thought, 'They looked pretty fresh to me,' and told him to show me his hands.

He stuck one hand in his pocket and showed me the other. I thought, 'You fucking twat, like I am going to be that stupid to go, 'Oh yeah, your hand looks fine, OK, go on in the pub!'

'Show me your other hand, dickhead.'

He pulled his hand out of his pocket and it was still weeping where he had just been fighting. I told him, 'You are not coming in tonight. Go home, your night is over.'

With that, he decided that that wasn't what he wanted to hear. His response was to punch me in the face. Fucking little twat. I ducked back. My colleague that was stood next to me caught him out of the corner of his eye and punched him full-on in the face. Now, my buddy could bench 200kg. He was strong. A 200kg punch to the face is no joke. It took him off his feet and he landed on the pavement face down. As we all stood there assessing the situation he jumped up on his feet with his nose splattered across his face and decided to start spitting blood all over us. As he was doing that, he made another beeline for me. As he was running towards me, I was trying to look for my radio. My first thought was to hit him with it. I couldn't find it, so I kicked him in the head instead.

Not the greatest move, but effective when someone is about to attack you. It was my first instinct. Use your feet. He fortunately ducked under my wrangler boot. It was like something out of The Matrix. All my team were there by then and they restrained him to the floor.

That could have been a normal punter inside the pub having

a drink, minding their business, and this asshole decides he wants to scrap. That's why you keep them out.

Another evening was the week before Christmas. I don't know what happens to people over Christmas. But these are some of the worst nights you can do on the door. It is like these people haven't been out all year. They come out over Christmas and decided they are allowed to behave exactly how they want and drink as much as they want. Even though they can't handle it, and just become complete and utter dickheads.

Scott had said, 'I'm not happy about there being only two of you working on the door.'

It was me and my mate Dave. Dave was pretty young, but he was super handy and I knew that he had my back.

I said, 'Stop fussing, we will be all right.' Off I went and arrived at the pub.

The funny thing about working in nightclubs and pubs is that when you arrive and walk into the place, you will always know what type of night you are going to have. There is an energy when you walk through the door.

The only reason there was only two door staff on, was because the manager was trying to save money.

When I walked through the door that night I knew instantly we were going to have trouble. I messaged Scott to get down as soon as he could.

There was a Christmas party in. It was a company that supplied marquee tents. The group consisted of big fat middle-aged men that were already pissed and playing up. I had gone over and asked one of them to get down off the furniture. He asked me to say the magic word. I then told him to get the fuck down off the furniture.

With that Dave had called me over to the gents toilet where

66

there was a cash machine. One of the men had smashed in the glass fronting to it, for no reason at all. He had to go.

Me and Dave were calmly walking him out. The rest of the group surrounded us and balled us out the doors of the pub onto the street. As I was being pushed out the door, one of the assholes punched me in the back of the head.

We were now both out in the middle of the street. I was on the pavement surrounded by six twenty-stone men. In my head I thought, 'Right, you are going to get the shit kicked out of you now.'

All I could think to do was make myself as small as possible. I tucked my head into my arms and waited for the onslaught. Dave saw this and managed to punch one of them in the head. He decided to do that to get them away from me . The six men then chased him into the road and decided to not only kick and punch him, but glass him as well.

Fortunately there were some marine friends of Dave's in the pub who saw what was going on and came out and helped us.

It was absolutely horrendous. These fucking assholes. The bar manager never helped. We were left on the front door to deal with the onslaught from the management of the company. They were holding me and Dave responsible for the situation, even though it was one of their employees that had smashed in the cash machine in the first place.

I should have sent Dave inside. He was fired up, and after you have had six men trying to put you in hospital, you are not going to be in the right frame of mind. One of the managers of the party was getting right in his face. Dave decided to headbutt him.

We were both pulled into the managers' office the following week, having to make an apology to these motherfuckers. They were never held accountable.

Scott arrived after the whole situation. I told everyone that he was not to be told what happened, as he would definitely go on a vigilante hunt to find them and do them in.

Around that time, Scott had been asked to step in at The Litten Tree to help with the Euro 2004 football championship. I'm not sure why I wasn't working in the pub then. The first night of the football championship that England had played, there had been a massive riot. The security had been left to deal with the chaos inside the pub, whilst the police stayed outside and watched. It was a shambles. The head doorman had asked Scott if he could come and be part of the team the following week. The team needed big handy men to work, as there was going to be a zero tolerance policy that night.

The night had gone pretty smoothly, until last orders. Pete was one of the doorman that was working that night, and he was renowned for being a gobshite when he didn't need to be. He would generally cause situations that would end up in big fights. Not the best person to be outside dealing with a shithead that was threatening to bottle somebody. What should have happened is that Pete should have locked the doors and ignored him. But no. Pete was outside having it out with this lad. This is when Scott stepped in. Scott should have pulled Pete inside and left the dickhead to it. The shithead decided that he was going to start on Scott. Scott, not wanting anyone to think that he was weak, went over and punched the fella in the face. By Pete's account, the punch was amazing. He said the fella's head looked like it span round like a whizzing top before he hit the floor.

Unfortunately for Scott, the fella was unconscious for thirty minutes! The police were called and Scott was arrested. He spent the night in the cells. Scott was charged with GBH. I didn't know at the time because he was doing a very good job at keeping it all under wraps and not giving me all the information. It wasn't until after the day in court that he told me that GBH came with a custodial sentence of six months.

The shithead that was threatening people with smashing a bottle in their heads had said that Scott had broken his jaw. Fortunately for Scott there was a doctor in the court that had said there was no way that the injury had been sustained the night that Scott had hit him. It was an injury he had sustained on another night.

The judge in the courtroom had said to Scott that she would not want that job on any night of the week in town, and that he was to be charged with ABH and a conditional discharge. No prison time was to be spent.

This did mean though that he had lost his licence. He could no longer work on the door. He now had a criminal record that he would have to disclose at every interview he went to. This meant that finding a job with any kind of earning potential was limited. Scott felt that he deserved better than he got.

Scott didn't really want to work for it though. Scott had no skills.

Living at the flat was tough. I was still paying the lion's share of everything, as well as trying to organise the mortgage payments for the studio flat that was still full of weed. The flat we were in was a nice looking place at face value. But the only heating it had was underfloor heating. It did nothing about heating the flat other than keeping your feet warm, I just couldn't afford to keep it on. It was so damp and cold. I acquired a Calor gas heater that stank of gas. When you sat in the living room in the winter, you could see your breath when you were watching TV, and because of the damp, the sheets on the bed were wet to get into. It was just so miserable.

The mould was out of control; all over my clothes, all up the walls. When I complained to the landlord, they sent round a surveyor who was a slippery cunt. I thought he was being friendly. He basically told me it was all my fault after he had surveyed the flat and questioned me for an hour. His advice was to have the heating on full blast and have all the windows open. I mean, what the actual fuck! Who lives like that? I know, I'll work my fucking ass off and then just chuck it all out the window.

I said, 'That's it,' to Scott. 'I cannot live in this and we cannot afford both of the places. The weed had to go. You have no idea what the fuck you are doing. We'll move into the studio flat.'

The landlord had even suggested it was the way we were living. It made me think like I had never lived in a house before. She even posed the question, 'How are you living?'

I had to take a second to think and say to myself, 'Fuck you, this place has no proper heating. It is all external walls with no insulation. I am not going to be made to feel bad.'

So that was that, we went over to the studio flat. I had never been over there before. It was literally across the street. Once we opened the front door, my heart sank. The whole place was a shithole. The men that had been in there supposedly taking care of harvesting the weed had clearly been using it to harvest their own. I started to cry. It was such a mess, and this was the place I was now going to be living in.

After winning the world title, my life was meant to change, to get better. Not take a nose dive into living in a shithole with a husband that was drinking all the time and didn't really want to work. I managed to get the flat cleaned and turn it into a space we could live in. I had three weeks to strip all the woodchip paper, which was a son of a bitch to get off. Fucking woodchip

70

wallpaper! I got flashbacks to our house in Noble Close in the '70s. Woodchip paper everywhere and pampas grass.

I was in the studio, in my underwear with a steamer trying to strip that motherfucker off the walls. Using that steamer was so hot! Why didn't I just leave it? Really, all I was doing was trying to polish a turd! Scott, if I rightly remember, maybe helped one day. I was in that shithole place for at least three weeks trying to get it to some sort of liveable place for me to be in. Scott did not give a shit. Scott was busy getting drunk, taking drugs, pumping steroids into his body and, as it turns out, this was the start of the first woman he had a fling with.

When we eventually moved into that studio, I thought, 'OK, this is a fresh start, a new place. Less stress with the money. It was only £250 a month. I was paying £1000 a month living in the other place as well as the £250. I will be £1000 better off.'

Maybe I could find my place of wanting to have sex with him again. Scott never tried to make me feel special or a desired woman. I was the replacement for his mother. I had married a man baby. Scott never took care of anything. Scott did not know how to take care of anything. His mother had done it all for him, until I came along. It took me a while to figure that one out.

He confessed to me that he had kissed another woman. He told me that he wasn't getting it from me so he went elsewhere. I felt ashamed. I blamed myself. It was my fault because I wasn't putting out.

He told me that he didn't want to do it. But he needed to do it. Why didn't I leave then?

That didn't make me want him more, it just pushed me further away. But I still felt responsible for him. I didn't have anywhere to go as well. We were in so much debt. How was I going to find the money to move into another flat. I certainly

71

wasn't strong enough to admit that I just didn't want to have sex with him. I thought everyone would judge me. Shame. The worst feeling of all.

Scott was doing a good job at chipping away at my self-esteem. You don't even realise it is happening. It is nothing big, and it would be difficult to name one incident where you realise that they are doing it. But before you know it, you think you are no good to anyone and that no one else will love you or want to be with you.

I hated it in that flat. It was an embarrassment to be living in that place. I never invited anyone around there, ever. Only two people came there. My mate Debs, and Hurrington, one of my Thai boxing students. That's it. I didn't want anyone to see it.

My saving grace at that time was the powerlifting. The powerlifting coach was putting me through my paces. Lifting heavy shit was really hard work. The sessions would last at least two hours, sometimes three. I would get back to the flat and have to sleep before I could get going again. PT work is pretty unsociable hours. You will be out early in the morning training your clients and then back out from four-ish until late at night.

It wasn't long into the training before my coach put me into my first competition. This meant I had another competitive outlet whilst I couldn't fight.

At that time, I was squatting 140kg, benching I think around 70kg, and deadlifting 140kg. At a powerlifting competition, you get three lifts for each discipline. You have to be super careful about picking what numbers you lift. Your first lift should really be your last warm up lift. See how you feel out on the stage in front of everyone and then make your decision on your next number. I don't remember what comp it was and didn't really think I did all that well. But apparently I got nine out of nine lifts and took silver. The coach was happy, and made a bit of a song and dance out of it. I let it all go over the top of my head. Get back into the gym, keep training, get stronger!

Scott at this point had decided that he didn't want to work as a care worker any more. He was going to work with his friend who, at that time, had not long come out of prison. This was the same friend that had given him the idea to buy the flat to grow weed in!

His mate, Lewis, let's call him, was building houses at that time. He is very skilful, but unfortunately also wanted the quick buck. Meaning, if he could come up with a plan to make money without having to really work for it, he would take any opportunity that came along, whether it was legal or illegal.

Scott was going to be a labourer on the site that Lewis was building the house on. Scott was big and strong. They would get him lifting and moving all the big shit on the site.

Scott had gone to work and I was sat in the studio, figuring out how we were going to pay the mounting debt that we had. Then I heard a fizzing noise coming from the trip switch box. It didn't sound right to me, but I thought, 'I'll wait until Scott gets home and ask him.'

I don't know why, because Scott was clueless. Anyway, I brought it up with him and he said, 'There is an electrician on site. I'll ask him.'

I left it for a couple of days, although the fizzing sound was getting worse. Of course, Scott hadn't talked to the electrician. I begged him again if he could ask him to come. His answer: 'Yeah, yeah, I'll ask him.'

After the third day, I was sat at home again studying when I noticed that the fizzing sound was getting worse when all the electrical appliances were on. It was making me nervous. I decided to switch the mains switch off in the trip switch box until I got home.

I walked through the door after coaching all afternoon to see that Scott was home. He had balanced the fridge-freezer on different sized saucepans. The fridge-freezer looked pissed! I said, 'What the fuck are you doing?'

'I'm trying to plug the fridge-freezer into a different plug to see if it works.'

The plug lead on the back of the fridge-freezer was really short. In Scott's mind, balancing the fridge-freezer on the saucepans would give it some height to reach the other plug socket.

I said, 'It's broken!' Something to do with the fizzing in the electricity box had blown it and now it was not working.

Scott decided to start shouting at me. His response was that at least he was trying to do something. I looked at him like he was a lunatic, because it made no sense to me. I know, I'll balance the fridge-freezer on saucepans that are different sizes, because that sounds right.

Scott then proceeds to take off the outer wooden box to the trip switches and poke the main transformer with a feather brush. His logic; using the plastic end of the brush because plastic is not a conductor. He then turns the main switch off and on again. I was still stood there thinking, 'What the fuck is this idiot doing?'

He then decided to get hold of the transformer and give it a shake. GIVE IT A SHAKE! 240 volts, I am to believe, coming through that transformer and he decided to give it a shake. He then turned the mains switch on again. We were now in the twilight zone. All the electrical appliances were switching on and off, lights, tv, computer. I then saw a blue flame coming out of the transformer. I said, 'Fuck this, you fuck off.'

I needed to think quick about what I was going to do about that situation. Scott fucked off out in a huff! I switched off the mains and sat there in the dark. It was about ten p.m. Who the fuck was I going to call? I decided to call British Gas, our energy supplier. That was the first thing that came into my head. I explained about the blue flame and said, 'What do I do?'

The man on the other end of the phone very calmly told me to get out of the house, and that it was really dangerous. I reassured him that nothing was on and that I was sat in the dark.

Within ten minutes I had a man at the door looking at the problem. Within five minutes there were another two men in the flat fixing the problem, and let me tell you – they were not using a feather duster to fix it!

This is what it was like living with Scott. It was one thing after another. I had fortunately had the foresight to get contents insurance. Thank goodness for that. Scott decided one night that he was going to do the washing up. I thought he was filling up the bath and the sound of the water I could hear was coming from the bathroom. But no, it was coming from the kitchen, because he decided that he would turn on the taps, put the plug in and go and sit down. I mean, how long does it take to fill up the kitchen sink with water? It certainly doesn't take the time to go and have a sit down on the couch for twenty minutes.

There was banging on our flat door. I opened it, and it was the neighbours from downstairs, telling me that water was pouring through their ceiling. I was like, 'What the fuck?' I ran into the kitchen to see the sink overflowing and the taps still running. Fuck my fucking life!

I was able to give them my insurance details and that took care of that!

Scott lasted three weeks as a labourer, until one day he came

75

home and announced that he wasn't going back to work. My immediate thought was, 'Fuck. How am I going to pay the bills?' I don't think I even challenged him on it. I might have said, 'OK you need to find another job,' but didn't really push it.

Scott never once thought about how we were paying the bills, eating or living! As long as I was working and paying for everything, why should he think about where the money was coming from? Scott just did what Scott wanted to do.

Scott never once wanted to take responsibility for his behaviour. I knew that he was lying to me about the drinking. He would tell me all the time that he was going to meetings. I knew that he wasn't. The lying would really fuck me off. I mean, this is an alcoholic. He should not be drinking, and the fact that he was doing it in secret made it even worse. It was the deceit that makes you feel like shit. How could he love me? The addiction always comes first.

It was around this time that he had start to question me on being a lesbian. He would say to me, 'You sure you're not a lesbian?'

I wasn't having sex with him, so therefore I must be a lesbian. Never mind that I was up to my neck in debt, and his drinking, lying, kissing other women, was making me generally feel like shit. Sure, Davis, just lay back and open your legs, that's all you've got to do. He would quite regularly say that to me. 'What's the matter with you? All you've got to do is lay back and open your legs.' Such loving and desirable words. Made me feel all woman.

He got himself a self-hypnosis book. I honestly think he thought he was going to hypnotise me, fucking idiot. I would get in from work and he would sit there on the bed doing this movement with his fingers. I would say to him, 'What the fuck are you doing? You are not going to hypnotise me!' He would give up and go out.

He had now moved on from the woman that he had kissed and was now sleazing around my friends, or my so-called friends.

I had stupidly gotten him a phone with a contract. What the fuck was I thinking? He ran up a £400 bill! How the fuck was I going to pay that? Of course, we had a massive argument. I took the phone off him and I went through the bill. There was a number that was repeated over two to three hundred times in the same bill. I phoned it. It was my old school friend, Natalie. I phoned her. 'What the fuck have you two been talking about?' She fobbed me off, giving me some shitbag story. I somehow found some of the messages. He had been telling her how much he loved her. Had they met up? Who knows? Had they fucked? Who knows?

That was the end of our friendship, I had known her since I was seven years old! I knew who he was. I trusted my friends to be my friends and tell him to fuck off when he started doing his shit.

I still didn't leave him.

I had my second powerlifting comp. It was in Taunton at a community centre. Just a little back-of-nowhere centre. I had turned up in my Machine Martial Arts T-shirt. When I weighed in, the woman told me that I had to turn it inside out. I asked, 'Why?'

'We don't allow any unofficial sponsoring.'

'It's just a t-shirt with my martial arts name on it. We are in the back of beyond with about thirty people watching.'

It wasn't even being televised or anything. It was just a small-bit comp.

She said, 'No, turn it inside out.'

I thought, 'That's absolutely ridiculous.'

I did well at the comp again; I can't remember what I lifted but I got nine out of nine lifts. Just when I was about to leave, I was approached by a UK doping official.

She said, 'You are to be tested for drug taking.'

It really took me by surprise. I was then to be chaperoned everywhere until I was able to take a pee. This is where a person stands in front of you while you piss. It is horrible, invasive and just a bit humiliating. I have never taken performance enhancing drugs. I remember getting really upset. I didn't like it one little bit.

Of course, the results were clear. This would happen to me at most lifting comps I went to. I just got used to it in the end. I'm not sure why I got singled out. I wasn't breaking any records or lifting numbers that were outstanding. They obviously decided that I looked like a type that needed to be tested all the time.

All the powerlifting and squatting was making me strong. Dave was talking about me fighting again. There was talk of going to Thailand again. The Bulldog and some of the Machine Martial Arts crew were talking about going as a group. I mentioned it to Scott. His response was, 'No way. I don't want to go. You'll end up getting caught for drugs and going to prison.' Scott had this paranoia about going to Thailand. He assumed that everyone that went there would end up getting planted with drugs and going to prison!

I said, ' Don't be so stupid! I want to go and I'm going. Come or don't come, I'm going.'

That set the wheels in motion for my comeback fight. I compromised and said kickboxing only, no Thai boxing because my knee wouldn't take it.

It was meant to be a five-round fight against a local girl. I think they thought that because 'The Machine' had been out of action for two years, she wouldn't be what she was. My ego was right up for it. Unfortunately, there were some politics that happened, and the local girl pulled out. Dave then said, 'Let's make this a European title fight.'

My ego said, 'Yes.' But my coach should have said, 'No.'

My coach should have suggested a couple of warm up fights to blow away the ring rust and then think about the European title fight. But no, Dave was a promoter and was thinking about the money he could make. I was caught up being Billy big bollocks. Of course I could do a European title fight. Dave wasn't looking out for me. So, that was that. European title fight set. Training commences. Thailand trip, here we come.

Whilst I had distanced myself from Dave. I was still going into the fight shop for validation. I don't know why. I know now that Dave didn't care. But I suppose I still wanted to feel like I was part of the team that he said that we were. I wanted to feel like I still belonged somewhere.

The Comeback Fight

It was August 2006, and Scott was not coming to Thailand. That was a definite. I was going and I was taking eight other of my Thai boxing buddies with me. I couldn't wait. Ten whole days without Scott. I had twelve weeks as a training camp to get myself ready to fight for the European title!

The whole group was so excited about going and being together on the journey. Three boys and five girls. The boys were eighteen, nineteen, and twenty-one. The eighteen-year-old's mum had asked me at Bournemouth coach station, 'Please do not let anything happen to him.'

I promised her that I would look after everyone!

We arrived at the Fairtex camp in Pattaya. Pattaya is very different from the island of Koh Samui where I had been before. It was very much more commercial. The Fairtex camp was great though. A gated community. You didn't really have to step off the site. You had everything you needed. We got ourselves settled in our rooms, went and looked at the training area and then got ourselves set up for the following morning, ready to hit some shit up.

I phoned Scott to let him know I was safe and to check in with him. Scott was pissed out of his head. He could barely string a sentence together. I came off the phone and just thought, 'You selfish cunt!'

At seven a.m. the following morning we were all up and ready to train. There is never a sense of urgency with the Thai trainers. They just laze around. You have to wait for them to be ready, even though you are paying for the privilege to be there.

I had been to Thailand before, so I knew how hot it was going to be. It was seven a.m. in the morning and the heat was already at thirty degrees. The training rings were all situated outside with a canopy over the top of them. I knew that the Thai trainers would pick the boys first, of course. Clearly, being the more supreme beings as males, they would go first in their training. Us girls were left to warm up and wait until they decided that they would train us.

I watched the boys in the ring and laughed a lot to myself. Six minute rounds on the pads. For six rounds. They were only ever used to doing two or maybe three minutes maximum and certainly not in thirty degree heat. One of the boys was hanging over the ropes at the end of one of the rounds having his head showered by a hose because he was dying from the work rate and the heat.

Going to Thailand to train is just the best trip for me. Sun, tick. Training, tick. Thai massage for a pound, tick. Eating amazing Thai food, tick. I mean, what else do you need from a trip abroad?

The Thai massage is unbelievable. There was a Thai massage parlour opposite the Fairtex camp. The whole troop took off together after training one evening. I was daydreaming at the back, as per usual. I was the last one through the door. The massage parlour had separated the boys from the girls. We were given pyjamas to put on. If you have never had a Thai massage in Thailand, they give you pyjamas to put on. You do not take your clothes off.

All these little light Thai women came out of this room and assigned themselves to each one of the group. As I was last through the door, I saw this heavy set Thai woman stomping her way down the corridor. I thought, 'Oh shit. If I get her, I am in trouble.'

Well, you know what happens; I do get her. She did not hold back either, she spent one whole hour beating the shit out of me. All the girls were laughing because it wasn't them that ended up with her. £2 later I felt like a new woman.

As we were all walking out, one of the boys was looking more pale than usual. He piped up as we were walking back and said that the woman he was assigned would not leave his dick alone, and spent the whole hour whispering sexual pleasantries in his ear. I mean, it's bloody awful, and had it been a woman getting that from a man, we would all be up in arms. But we all just laughed. He said he spent the whole time trying not to get a hard-on and thinking about inane objects like lightbulbs and other power tools to get himself through it. Super funny. But also very bad, very bad indeed.

Every evening, I would phone back to the UK to check in with Scott. On every phone call I made, Scott was drunk off his face. I felt guilty because I wasn't at home. I think I felt responsible again for him drinking himself to death. It did certainly put a taint on the trip. But I made sure I got up every day, trained, laid in the sun and tried to enjoy the trip as much as I could.

The boys appeared at breakfast one morning covered in glitter. I asked them what they had been up to.

Nothing was shared and nothing was ever spoken about. I sat there laughing. They didn't need to share. I knew what they had been up to.

One of the Thai coaches had taken them out to a strip bar. I think one of the boys got pulled up on the stage and stripped bare.

I sat there watching them starry-eyed from what had happened the night before. It was funny. I giggled on the inside. I was well aware of what had happened, so they didn't need to explain. What happens in Thailand, stays in Thailand!

Mum was back on the scene. It had been twelve years since I had seen her. She had not bothered to try and find me and Leigh, nor had she made any effort to see how we were, how we were getting on. I find that all very strange for a parent.

Me and Leigh had been contacted by a family friend. Apparently, Mum had cancer and we were to go and see her. My initial thought was, 'Fuck her! She never bothered with us, why should I now just because she is my mum? Why should I do right by her now because she is ill?'

Leigh phoned me, 'What do you want to do sis?'

I said, 'I fucking knew this would happen!'

Either one of them was going to get ill and we were now meant to step up and look after them.

I said, 'Right, this is what we are going to do. You and me, Leigh, we are good people. We will go together and see her, because it is the right thing to do. But if she starts any of her shit, we are out of there!'

Leigh's response was, 'All right, sis I'm right with you. you leave, I leave!'

Mum had breast cancer and had just come out of her surgery. She certainly wasn't terminal. Unfortunately for her she developed it through bad lifestyle choices and not looking after herself. It is not genetic. We do not have cancer on either side of the family. The doctors told her it was diet related.

Me and Leigh turned up together. It was weird and stilted. She was kind of happy to see us. She passed a comment on how I looked with my muscles. We stayed for a while. I gave her my number. Told her to ring me to arrange to see her again.

She never mentioned the time we hadn't seen each other. Didn't really ask me what I had been doing. Just carried on like nothing had really happened. I went with her to the hospital and spent time with her changing her eating habits, changing all the toiletries she used to make sure they were chemical free. Just spent time with her whilst she went through her treatment and aftercare.

This was while I was training for my European title fight.

I had to drop weight again to 66kgs. I needed to be this to fight. I walk around comfortably at 80kgs. That is my natural weight. I can drop to 75kgs. That is not too much of a push, but 66kgs is too light for me. However, as my coach told me before, 'You either want it or you don't.'

So 66kgs was what it was.

Leading up to the fight, Mum's input was, 'You're too skinny.'

I responded, 'This is what it is. I'm fighting and this is how it is going to be.' I just ignored her because she knew nothing about getting ready to fight. The usual story, nothing positive.

I made weight without too much stress. 66kg. I was back and ready to fight.

It was weird being back. I just didn't feel like I belonged. I was with supposed friends, but they weren't my friends. I knew they were all talking shit about me behind my back and being nice to my face. I hate that shit. I'd rather someone tell me that they don't like me, and I know where I am, than all the fake bullshit to my face. My relationship with Dave had fallen apart. I wasn't part of The Bulldog team as it was. I really didn't have a great deal of respect for him. I was at the fight because of my ego!

Fighting gives you notoriety. You are respected for getting into the ring. It gives you focus and discipline. The majority of people that get into fighting generally come from challenging backgrounds. It is a way out of the dysfunction that surrounds them. Unfortunately, when their fighting career is coming to an end, most fighters lose their way with trying to normalise their life away from the fighting career. They will question who they are. They will question their identity because, without the training and the fighting, they believe that they are nothing. That's why you see so many of them getting back in the ring. The adoration, the belonging. The crowds. The feeling of being in the ring.

Not having a skillset when you leave any kind of athletic career that has outlined your identity will definitely mean you will spiral out of control. Turn to drink and drugs. Spiral into a depression. You need another outlet, a focus to keep yourself intact.

It was time for me to fight. I was top of the bill again. I'm not sure how many people were there to see me fight. There were at least one thousand five hundred people there. Dave had really bigged up the night. There was expectation on my performance. I go to the middle of the ring. The ref is talking to both of us. I, as usual, am not listening to a word of it. I am looking straight into the eyes of my opponent. I am making sure she understands that I am there to fight and that she had better be ready. The bell goes, first round.

The strangest thing happens in that first round. I am having an internal conversation with myself. I ask myself, 'What am I doing there?' I say to myself, 'I don't want to do this any more.' I thought, 'I'll just get out of the ring and leave.'

I was literally going to walk over to the ropes and get out of the ring.

Whilst this internal conversation is happening, I am fighting automatically, unconsciously. It's so weird.

I suddenly come back to awareness and I realise I am right in the middle of the first round and there are people there watching me. I can't get out the ring and if I don't get my shit together, she is going to knock me out.

Right, my only option now is to fight and fight like I don't want to lose.

Second round in and my opponent clips me under my right eye. It starts to swell. When I'm sat in the corner at the end of the round the doctor is straight in to have a look. He asks me if I can see. I suddenly thought, 'Oh, this could be my way out. Do I lie?'

But then I saw Dave looking straight at me. He didn't say it out loud, but I knew he said don't even think about it. I said, 'Yes, yes I can see!'

The fight went on for another five rounds. At the end of the fifth round, the skin was starting to split under my eye in the eye socket. The doctor called it. He said the fight was over.

I had never been so relieved. Dave went and checked the score cards. He said I had won every round up until that point. But because the doctor stopped it, it went to the other fighter.

I didn't care. I wanted out. I never wanted to be back in the ring ever again. Certainly not with Dave in my corner. I felt like I fought that fight on my own. I had no connection to those people with me. It was a massive epiphany. My fight career was over.

Scott was there that night, completely off his head on ecstasy and vodka. I could hear his voice when I was in the ring above everyone's. Apparently the security, along with the rest of the crowd were busy watching him, because he was so wasted. Never mind being there to support me. Once again it was all about him.

Being responsible for him. Taking care of him.

My mum turned up as well. I didn't really want her there either. She was fussing around me when I was in the warm up area after the fight. I just did not care one bit about the fight. I did not care that I lost. I went over at the end of the fight and shook my opponents hands. I was out of there!

It was so empowering. I was done. All I wanted to do now was lift big heavy weights. Get strong, see where I could go with that. I had my new outlet, my new focus, my new discipline.

The New Journey

All I wanted to do was go home and just be still. My head was banging. My eye was massive. I was so over all of it. I was waiting by the car and Scott was so fucking high. I thought, 'You selfish cunt. I am going to have to drive us home.' There was no chance that I could sit back and chill after being battered around the ring for five rounds.

There was one of Scott's friends loitering around by the car. I was just about to get in when Scott said, 'Get in mate.'

I said, 'What the fuck is going on?'

'Can we give him a lift home?'

'I just want to go home, I looked at him with disdain, I'm fucked!'

Now I am driving this fucking dude to the other side of town because that selfish cunt has said that he would give him a lift home. I should have put my foot down and said no. But me being me, I drove him to his house and then drove both of us home.

From that point on I have never questioned getting in the ring again. I knew that that journey was done.

My head was in a different place. I had started competing in power lifting and it turned out I was pretty good at it.

Mum was doing well with her recovery and I was trying hard to build a relationship with her. I knew who she was and I was stronger and in a different emotional place. I was secure with who I was, and thought that I could handle her and her mental instability.

Not long after the fight I was round her house on a quick visit. She had asked to borrow the DVD of the fight. I didn't think anything of it. I said, 'Sure!', and gave her a copy. The next time I went round to visit, she played the fight back to me in slow motion and told me everything I was doing wrong!

I remember just looking at her and thinking, 'Are you for real?'

I just watched her. I thought, 'Nothing has changed. You are never going to be in a place where anything positive can come out of your mouth that is of any good. No praise, no well done, no recognition of any kind of bravery it takes to get in the ring and get smashed in the face. No, you just want to point out everything that was wrong!'

My mum, before my last fight, had never seen any one of my fights, EVER! She had never followed me in any of my training. She had never invested in anything that I have done for myself. She came to ONE fight and decided that she was going to tell me what I had done wrong. Un-fucking-believable!

I was existing in the studio flat from day to day. The place was so depressing, and we were in so much debt. I was in constant telephone calls with debtors that were trying to tell me that I was spending too much money on my food shopping bill.

Scott was busy not working and generally getting himself pissed, taking whatever drugs he could get hold of at the time. His choice of drug at that time was GHB.

GHB is not funny. You take too much, your heart stops. You die. Simple. But he and his friend were doing a lot of it. Apparently if you take it when you have been drinking and you get breathalysed, the alcohol limit will not show up in the test. Scott's buddy was being pulled over all the time and was always passing the tests. The police knew he was out of it but couldn't do anything because the test results would come back negative. Scott's mate did end up driving his car in the mid-morning into a shop window. He was lucky he did not kill anyone!

Scott did confess to me that there were numerous occasions that he had come home in the morning after being out all night with his mate that he was able to keep his shit together while I was there. But once I was out the door, he was rolling around on the floor in and out of consciousness. Twat!

The thing is, I knew he was getting wasted. I just didn't care. If he was out, he wasn't bothering me. I needed to work and try and get myself out of the horrendous debt situation I was in.

The first of the threats to leave him came around this time. I know I pushed for him to get back to his meetings. He would leave me letters all the time, promising to do better, to be better. 'Please don't leave me!' I wouldn't necessarily fall for it, but I would always give him the benefit of the doubt. I realise now I was just being played. He never did anything about being better. He never wanted to. I fell for the promises every time! Such an idiot. You believe this person does care for you. It was like being on a merry-go-round. He hurts you; the trust has been broken. I don't want him to touch me. You give it time to see if he can do better. That might last for a moment and then something else happens, and you are right back where you started. Hating him and all the shit that comes with living with a narcissistic addict.

This was my life. Living with a narcissist means that everything will revolve around them. It will be all about their needs, their wants, their life. Nothing will ever be their fault. Even with evidence to the contrary, it is still never their fault. The narcissist will neglect you; they will take you for granted and never make you feel important or valuable. Selfish is an understatement when you are dealing with them. A narcissist lacks empathy and compassion, and the only feelings they care about are their own. Everyone around a narcissist is an object to them to be used for their own gratification or needs.

Scott came home one day and said that he had been to an audition to start an evening class in acting. He mentioned that everyone that was there was around eighteen to twenty. They all thought he was a parent. He performed a monologue from a famous playwright. I can't remember who it was. But the tutor that was assessing the auditions said to him at the end, 'Clearly you can act. Do not waste your time with this evening class. I will put you forward for a BA in Theatre Studies at Bournemouth University.' He did come home and question whether or not he should be doing it. But I supported him and said he could not pass up this opportunity.

So that was that for the next three years. I justified again the fact that he wasn't working because he was at Uni studying!

Machine Martial Arts was going really strong. I started at Fitness First Health Club. It was me and mine. I did find it hard to leave The Bulldog though. To really separate myself from them. I would find myself in the gym or the fight shop seeking confirmation of what I was doing. Silly really. Truly, 'The Bulldog team' that sat in that back office on their ivory towers thinking that they were better than anyone else did not give one shit about me and what I was doing!

My classes were going really well and it wasn't long before I had my own fight team developing.

I had my first fight night in Southampton to go to with two fighters that I had trained under Machine Martial Arts. Billy was twenty-one and a know-it-all, especially in sessions. I would set up a drill to do and he would always be doing something different. When I questioned him on it, his response was always that he felt that what he was doing was better. Just an upper middle-class kid that was used to getting what he wanted and thinking that he knew best. It used to wind me up a treat. My response was always, 'Just do what I have fucking asked you to do. There is a reason that I have set the drills. Have you ever had a fight in your life? NO, that's right, you haven't. I have, and quite a few. I know that this drill works, so just fucking do it, or just fuck off.'

That always seemed to get through to him. He wanted to fight and I felt that he was at a level where he could have his first fight. Jason was another fighter that was ready. He was just difficult to manage. He would turn up in the morning for sprint training on the beach with a bag of skittles for pre-training nutrition. Of course, that would do my nut in as well. But I knew that he could bang, and bang hard. He was ready for his first fight too.

We arrived at the hall where the fight event was happening for the weigh-in. Billy weighed in on target. Jason was a fucking embarrassment. I told him what he needed to be and he kept reassuring me that he was on target. Jason got on the scales and was at least 4kg over. Now, it doesn't sound like a lot, but fight promoters and trainers can get really funny about making weight. The guy weighing him in said, 'He's going to have to find a sauna somewhere and lose some water.'

Jason got a fucking bollocking from me! My first trip out, and he's making me look like a fucking idiot. I could see two men at the bottom of the table where we were weighing in. They were both watching and laughing. Jason hadn't seen them, but I did. I had a sneaky suspicion that one of them was Jason's opponent. I told Jason to fuck off and get out of my sight. I looked at the men and thought, 'Yeah, fuck you. You'll know once Jason gets in the ring.'

I took Billy out the back in the warm up area until we were ready to go on.

I started to get this overwhelming feeling that Billy was going to get the shit kicked out of him. I couldn't show him that though. I started to warm him up. I could tell he was really nervous. I kept reassuring him. Just before we were ready to go out, I told him, 'I do not care how hard it gets for you in there. You are going to fight out of your skin today. You will at no point be getting out of that ring, do you understand me?' Billy looked at me straight in the eyes and nodded his head.

Billy climbed into the ring. I told him it was game time and to get his shit together. The bell went, and Billy was doing really well. Then all of a sudden, he takes a hit that puts his ass through the ropes. He looks straight across to me. I scream at him to get the fuck up and fight. Billy gets up and makes it to the end of the first round. I sit him down. Give him a little chat. Billy goes out for the second round. He holds his own and makes it through the round. I knew Billy wasn't going to win this fight, but that didn't matter. My job was to make sure that he made it through to the end of the third round. If I threw the towel in, he would carry that for the rest of his life. Billy goes out for the third round. He is starting to fatigue. He takes two standing counts but keeps on fighting. The bell goes and that is the end of the fight. I was so proud of him. Billy never fought again, but he will always have the respect for himself that he never gave up. He did tell me after the fight that he was more afraid of getting out the ring and facing me than the fight itself. I said, 'I did what it took to get you through that fight.'

Jason was back from finding a sauna. He still wasn't on weight but the promoter decided that he would take it because he was probably depleted from sitting in heat for an hour. Never a great way to prepare on the day of your fight!

We literally had minutes to warm up. We walked out to the ring and waited for his opponent to get in. I was right. One of the men that were laughing at us when we were weighing in was Jason's opponent. I really didn't need to say much to Jason. I knew that he was a fighter and I knew that when Jason started to punch his opponent in his face that it would be a game changer.

Jason stopped his opponent in the second round. I went over and shook their hands and then stood in the corner laughing at them. Fucking twats. They thought my fighters were going to be pushovers because they were trained by a woman. Well, they found out different.

The promoter phoned me the following day and praised me on how I trained my fighters and how well they did. I thought that was really nice. It reaffirmed myself as a trainer and how I was training my students.

Lifting Is My Church

Of the many cars that we owned when I was married to Scott, one that was purchased was a people carrier. Scott never looked after the cars we had and they were always breaking down. We never had the money to fix them.

One day, when he was driving home along the Wessex way – a dual carriageway – the car started to smoke. Instead of pulling over to see what was happening, he decided that he would stick his head out of the window to drive, so that he could see, because the whole car was filling up with smoke. He managed to get back and park outside of the flat where there just so happened to be a fire engine on the other side of the road.

Scott jumped out of the van and pulled open the sliding door, only for an abundance of McDonald's wrappers and used food bags to fall out onto the road. Along with parking tickets that he had been hiding under the car seat. He was such a messy fucker.

A fireman walked across the road and said, 'You know your car is smoking?'

In his kerfuffle of looking like he was dealing with the situation his response was, 'Yeah, I know.'

I think the fireman gave him a strange look and slowly walked away.

The van was a death trap, and there was no way I was going to drive it any more. I hadn't realised how many parking tickets there were as well. Instead of dealing with them he would just hide them.

The car was in my name. I had to make sure of that. Otherwise, he would be driving around with no tax or insurance. They wouldn't be chasing him for the tickets, they would be chasing me. Parking ticket debt collectors are one hundred percent complete and absolute fucking assholes.

Along with trying to organise payment to all the debt companies, I now had to sort out paying a £1000 parking ticket fine for the number of tickets he had accumulated. Which was a fucking nightmare.

I tried to ask for a payment book so at least I could try and pay it off in small payments. Whilst on the phone to this asshole, the collector told me that I needed to get a loan. I remember I was just about to start training a client at the gym. I couldn't believe what I was hearing! I mean, how was I supposed to get a loan? I had zero credit!

Let's have it right, as well. Those parking tickets start out at £25, and if they are not paid within fourteen days they double or even triple. If by then they haven't been paid, you will be looking at £100 a ticket.

When you are in so much debt, the parking ticket becomes the least of your worries. Yes, you should pay it straight away. But you have so many companies breathing down your neck, sending you aggressive, threatening letters, that you just put them at the bottom of the pile.

I had to put the phone down on the collector. I told him I would ring him back once I had gotten my head around what he had just said to me. Once I had a moment, I phoned him back. His response to me was, 'If you ever put the phone down on me again, I will be round your house so fast to strip it out that I wouldn't have time to think.'

These people that you are dealing with work for your local

council! What a complete and utter fucking arsehole. I told him that he couldn't speak to me that way. I was trying to work a payment out. I wasn't trying not to pay it. He could at least come to some kind of arrangement. This arsehole, though, wasn't having any of it. He wanted his money and that was that.

My next plan was to go to Citizens' Advice. I needed to know my rights. Three hours out of my day going down to the bureau to see what I could do. I had told Scott. He decided to go to the police station. He asked the policeman behind the counter if he could kick the debt collector in the legs. He informed the police officer that he knew he couldn't punch him in the face but maybe he could kick him in the legs instead. The policeman's response was that it was a civil matter, and they would have nothing to do with them. Scott then answered with, 'Well, I'm just telling you that I am not going to let them take my car away from me.'

He then left the station.

I'll tell you what I thought: 'If you had, number one, parked in a space where you did not accumulate so many fucking tickets and, number two, paid for the tickets, I would not have been in that position of trying to sort out a bullshit aggressive parking ticket debt collector!'

The very nice gentleman at Citizens Advice, let's call him Paul. Basically told me that I had to try and get rid of them quick smart. I then told him that the debt collector had threatened me with coming into my home and taking everything I owned. I gave him the number, and Paul phoned the debt collector and tried to negotiate with him. The debt collector then turned on Paul, started to threaten him also.

The conversation turned pretty heated, because the debt collector was a fucking piece of shit!

97

I left Citizens' Advice with nothing in place really. So much time wasted sorting out Scott's bullshit. I went home and tried to forget about it for that day.

I did manage, the following day, to arrange a payment of £200 to pay towards the £1000 owed. The rest was paid off in increments.

In amongst all the madness I was lifting heavy shit. A lot of heavy shit. Lifting was my church, my place where I could forget about Scott, the debt, the chaos. I could find some peace. I was competing pretty much every other month. It was brutal. The competitions would be a bit of a trek to go to. I would be up at four a.m. to travel on the same day as the comp. I was only getting one day off a week, as I was working the other six days. So, my only day off would be spent competing.

Training was my escape. It was my sanctuary from the craziness that was Scott. But the four a.m. starts were starting to kill me a bit. It would be three weeks sometimes, back-to-back before I had a day off, and forget about holidays, I could never afford to take time off. The only trip away I had around that time was Thailand. Scott never had any money to do anything and I certainly didn't have any spare cash around, after paying for all the debt, to go away. One year was turning into another year, and then another year, and another year. It was flying past so quickly it was scary. The end of the year would come around and I would wonder where it had gone. The only enforced time I would have off would be Christmas, because no one was around to train. Then the new year would start all over again, and I would think, 'OK, this year is going to be different.' I would make plans at the beginning of the year, but they would all just fall apart. Scott's behaviour never changed. The chaos just continued like a conveyor belt of shit.

Out of the Hell Hole, into the New

Machine Martial Arts was doing well. I had three adult sessions a week now, and two kids' sessions. I had fighters and I was grading the kids. I did keep a level of contact with Dave so that I could buy kit from his store but I didn't have any respect for him. He asked me one day, 'Are you making any money?' I found that question weird. Why would I be doing anything if I wasn't making any money. Maybe he assumed that I couldn't do it without him, who knows. He then informed me about his £25,000.00 BMW that he had just bought. Money and wealth and possessions has never impressed me, ever! I, again, thought that was weird. He finished the conversation off with how many 'friends' he had on Facebook! I mean, who the fuck cares about that? I certainly don't. I wasn't one of his friends that was for sure. I certainly wasn't asking to be friends with the him, let's have it real. The people on Facebook, they're not real, they are not your friends. They are all acquaintances you have made in your life. Most of them you don't even speak to.

I knew what he was doing. He was gloating. I just thought, 'Dick!'

An opportunity at this time came up for Scott to sell the studio. He also had a friend that had just renovated a flat. I went and had a look. It was amazing compared to where we were.

It was an attic flat. It had so much character. It had sloped ceilings, it felt cosy and fresh and new and just so much better than the shithole I had been staying in for the last eighteen months. There was a main bedroom with an en-suite, a long hallway, another small bedroom, another toilet room, and a little galley kitchen attached to an open plan living space. I wanted out of the shithole and I wanted into this place. It did mean paying more rent each month than what we had been paying, but I was done in that studio. Enough was enough.

It was another fresh start. We would have a bit of money to pay for the rent for six months. I thought it could give us a chance to work and get some money behind us. Give us a head start!

I always held out hope that things would change. That Scott would get better.

Moving day was eventful. Mum had loaned me her van, which was very helpful. But this van was like the half sized vans. Not a big white van. So trying to fit in the bed, sofa and all our belongings was going to prove tricky. It was going to take a few trips.

We were stood just outside the van trying to figure out the mattress. It wasn't quite going in right. We had the side door open and I just moved him out of the way with my shoulder. Scott then shoved me into the van. I went in head first! I jumped out. I said to him, 'What the fuck are you doing?'

His response was, 'Don't push me out the way!'

I shoved him back. His response was to grab me. I responded by putting him in a head lock. We are now full on wrestling on the pavement outside of the van. Anyone watching us must have thought, 'What the fuck are those two up to?' An eighteen-stone, muscle bound man, with a woman who at the time was around eleven and a half stone, wrestling in the street.

In hindsight this type of behaviour is not normal. I didn't give it a second thought. My first thought was to fight back. I was a fighter. I was used to the physicality of being pushed around, of men hitting me and asserting their dominance over me. I was dealing with that every day in the gym. Of course, it is not normal, and I should not expect that from my partner that is supposed to love me.

The wrestling finished and we got ourselves together. I sorted out the mattress so that it fitted correctly and we took off to our new flat. It was like the ten minutes of physically wrestling each other in the street before hadn't actually happened. We sat in the car and didn't mention anything about it. I just wanted out of the shithole, so getting our furniture out of there and in to our new place was the only thing on my mind.

I was now lifting some big weights for me. I was squatting around 160 kgs, benching 80kg and deadlifting 170kgs. I was doing really well. I was definitely on course to start training with the GB powerlifting team. That was my main driving force. Making it to the team and starting to compete internationally again. I was training with my coach Pete three times a week, and the rest of the time I was doing all my extras that I needed to do to make sure I was covering all my bases. I didn't want to miss anything. Once I am committed to something I will give it one hundred and fifty percent of my effort to achieve.

I was also at this time, cycling everywhere. We had one car. Scott used the car most of the time. I did get the car in the evening to go out to work. I also did want to include the cycling into my weekly routine but it is much nicer when you can have a choice. We had no choice. I could not afford to run two cars. I paid for the tax, insurance, petrol. Scott never put petrol in the car. One of the biggest bugbears of mine, in amongst many, was that he would always run out of petrol. He just couldn't be bothered ever to put petrol in the car, ever! He certainly would never consider if I may need petrol to get to work. I would get in the car and the petrol gauge would always be on empty. Such a selfish prick.

So, bike it was. It took me a good twenty minutes to get to the main gym I worked at in the morning. Then I would spend the rest of the day charging around on my bike, taking care of everything I had to take care of.

I would pray for dry days. Many a time I would get up in the morning and look out the window to see rain, and my heart would sink. So miserable starting your day that way.

I had started asking at Fitness First if I could get a PT position. I needed a different outlet to work out of. I did have The Bulldog. But The Bulldog didn't have any gym equipment, other than the bags and pads to use. I was working in a gym in the back of Boscombe, which is a suburb over from Bournemouth town centre. It was a great gym, but there was new management that had taken over who were not my cup of tea at all. They were assholes, and I didn't want to give them my money.

I had been teaching my Thai boxing classes at Fitness First for a while now. I made friends with all the management, and asked one day if I could get a position there as a PT. It just so happened that they had an opening, and I landed myself a job as a PT at Fitness First. The footfall of traffic in the gym was more than where I had been working, and before I knew it, I was full of more clients. Which was just as well because Scott was still finishing his degree, and still not working.

One evening, after finishing teaching my Thai boxing session, we were driving home, I had decided to stop at Asda in Bournemouth. We needed some food and I wanted something for my dinner. As we were leaving Asda and walking into the car park, a car was skidding around at speed, and behaving so irresponsibly that a woman who was walking with her child had to grab them in order for them not to be run over. Seeing that incensed me. As the car parked, which was very close to where we were parked, I started to shout a few things at them, 'You might want to slow down a bit, you fucking idiots!'

I can say what I want to say and leave it at that. Scott, on the other hand, cannot. I, for a brief moment had forgotten that he was with me. Four young Asian looking men, who weren't very big, probably around five foot six at a push in height and definitely no heavier than ten stone, started to pull themselves out of the car. They were aggressive and were one hundred percent looking for trouble. They made a bee line for Scott.

'What you going to do about it, big man?'

As they approached us both, Scott walked towards them. I was carrying all the shopping. I wasn't about to shy away. I started to walk towards them. Scott told me, 'Get in the car!'

I ignored him. There were a few words exchanged. The Asian guys walked off. Scott got in the car. We were just about to leave the car park, when Scott stopped the car all of a sudden, and told me to go home! He then took off running across the car park after the young men.

Of course, I was not going to leave him there. It was like being in a Starsky and Hutch movie. I, skidded the car around, pulled it up close to the entrance of Asda. All I could see was Scott fighting four Asian men, and him getting smashed around the head with something that they had in their hands. Whether it was a phone or a weapon that they were carrying, who knows.

I ran up towards the entrance. I threw a kick at one of them. Three of them took off running. There were people there shopping just stood watching this all play out. Thankfully it was around nine thirty at night, which meant it was a bit quieter.

I ran inside and Scott was stood in front of one of these assholes. This asshole was goading him. He was stood outside the McDonald's that is just right inside the main doors of Asda in Bournemouth. He knew there was a camera there. Scott thought for a brief second, and then let one of his right hook punches go. He landed it flush on this guy's chin. The guy's head moved to one side. He did not drop. He then took off running.

I know for a fact that these guys were high on cocaine or PCP. There is no way that a ten stone guy can take a hit like that from a eighteen stone guy as strong as Scott was and walk away from it. It was crazy.

By the time we got out into the car park, they were gone. I said, 'The first thing we do is go to the police to report it. Get there first, just in case it comes back to bite you in the ass. We then get to the hospital.'

Scott's eye looked bad. His eye was completely dilated, with a nasty cut above it. His hand had a nasty cut in it, from the guy's teeth!

Oh, to be the fly on the wall when that guy came down from whatever drugs he was on and saw the state of his jaw.

The competing at the weekends was really starting to take its toll now. I was up to my neck in work trying to get a head of the bills. Trying to train five or six days a week, as well as cycling everywhere. I woke up one Sunday at four a.m. and just said I'm not doing it. I just can't have another two weeks of no days off. Emotionally, I was frayed. I phoned, said I am not coming and got back into bed.

When I went back to train with my powerlifting coach, he seemed all right. But then I soon realised that, rather than being straight with me and telling me that he was disappointed, he had started to send the other women forwards for GB selection and not me. I was lifting three times as a much as those women I was training with. I couldn't understand it. Why wasn't I being put forward? I realised then that I was being punished.

I kept training for a while, but I was so unhappy going there that I decided that it was time for me to leave. I had enough shit going on without being put through shit where I was training.

I decided to go and tell my coach to his face that I would not be training there any more. I told him that I was unhappy and that I didn't understand how I was being over looked over the women that I was training with. I was lifting three times as much as them. He took it pretty well at the time. That was until I got home, when he decided to call me and inform that maybe it was the pretty girl thing that I hadn't been put forward, and maybe it was my age! He had delivered that information in such a passive aggressive way. It wasn't until I got off the phone that I had realised that he had insulted me. You don't realise that you are being insulted until you have walked away from those types of conversations. I was fuming! How the fuck dare he? He was implying that I was not pretty enough and that I was too old. I went around and told everyone what he had said. I mean everyone!

Bournemouth is a small town, so it wouldn't have taken long for that to get back to him. He went out of his way to come and find me at Fitness First to apologise, stupid old twat.

There was another club I could go to. This club lifted in an affiliation that was untested. I didn't care. I just wanted to lift. To be honest, I knew where I was in this lifting organisation. The previous lifting club frowned upon this club because there were people that used steroids. The crazy thing about it is that the IPF that is supposedly drug free, which is why you get tested. You compete against people all the time that are taking drugs because they find ways to cheat the system. That just used to wind me up. Why not just go and lift in the other organisation where you can take drugs?

At least in this new organisation I knew where I was. I knew I was competing against drugs. That was my choice and their choice to do so. Taking drugs one hundred percent helps you with your training. It gives you the ability to get into the gym the day after a really heavy lifting day feeling fresh and ready to go, meaning your recovery time is shorter. Without drugs, I would have to take a couple of days rest in order to be able to keep going. Can you beat the drugs users? I say yes. You are about to find out.

Becoming a World Champion Again

Now, thankfully, Scott was finishing his degree. Scott had grand ideas that he was going to make it as an actor. He immersed himself in all the actors' agencies, and joined everything he could to be in that community. I was now paying for Scott to go to auditions. There were train tickets, food, etc. It was not cheap, and he certainly didn't have the money to pay for it!

During this time, Scott was also coming to a lot of my Thai boxing sessions. It wasn't long before him and his weed selling mate were looking to be set up for fights. I managed everything. I cornered him. I organised the day to make sure that it ran as smoothly as it could. People would often ask if I found it difficult to see him fighting. I never really thought about it, to be honest. I had a role to play and that was making sure that he was as prepared as he could be getting into the ring. Once you are in the ring it is your journey and your fight. You either win or your lose. Either way, I was there to pick up the pieces whatever the outcome was.

There is no way that Scott could have done that for me. He just didn't have the strength of character to do that for me. Scott did come to some of my lifting days. He was never a great support. The day would become about him and how bored he was, or how pissed up he was.

My first British Powerlifting Championship with the BPC was at the Bournemouth International Centre. Scott was drunk, drunk, drunk! He turned up late. I was just getting ready to go out on the stage to lift. Other than breathing his vodka breath in my face, he was of no help at all. I had to tell him to get the fuck out of my face. Fortunately, some friends stepped in and helped me get ready. Such a piece of shit. If the day wasn't about him he would just be an absolute arsehole.

On that same day, my previous powerlifting coach turned up to watch the competition, the one that decided to punish me. I courteously said hello, and then just got on with my day. I was told by my friends that were in the crowd that he was telling everyone that I was his lifter. So fucking sad. He punished me and I had to leave because of him, and now he is at a competition telling everyone that I am his lifter. I will never understand some people!

Nevertheless, I won that day. The memories of the weights I lifted are blurred but I won and it felt good.

Even though I was the winner, I was dragging a loser by my side. Scott had now finished his degree. There was no way he was not going to sit around doing fuck all. He had to get a job. He decided to return to care work. Everyone would think he was such an amazing person for working with the elderly or disabled. For the most part he was very good with them. But let's not get this twisted: the work suited his sluggish physical needs.

Some of the stories that he would tell me were so sad. Some of the elderly people that he would look after were left in their homes to rot and die. The carers are given a thirty-minute window to get them up, get washed and get fed. They are then left in front of their tv's for the day. The carer then goes back in the evening to repeat the morning and they are then put back into bed. Wash, eat, watch tv, sleep, repeat!

Scott would say that some of them were so desperate for a chat, but he just didn't have time because he had to get on to the next client.

There was one girl with locked-in syndrome and the only way they could communicate was through moving her eyes left or right. Scott would have to hold up a word sheet for her to spell out what it was she wanted to communicate, and when on form, he was patient and funny. Like I have said before he was good at his job, but his drinking and drug taking had really started to accelerate when we moved into the new flat.

There was no way of getting ahead with money. By the time the six months' rent had come to an end, we were right back where we started. Me, having to pay for everything.

Scott brought home around £250 a week and our rent was £750 a month. Put council tax on top of that, £115 gas and electric, £120 petrol, £120 insurance for contents because he was such a liability, income tax, etc. My food bill was around £160 a week. Massive debts to pay. The stress was through the roof for me. From one day to the next was just about survival.

Somehow, and I don't know how, I was sort of staying on top of things. I had decided to bin off his debts. They were his debts, not mine. They had his name on them. I was not sorting them any more. I concentrated on sorting my own financial situation. It was going to take years and years, but I was now in control of my shit and not his!

I challenged him about making more money. He would say to me, 'What's your problem? I'm bringing home £250 a week!'

My response would be, 'Our shopping bill is £160 a week motherfucker!'

I was left to pick up the rest of the slack. The arguments were getting uncontrollable, and this is when the physical violence took another notch up!

I can't even remember what we were arguing about, but we

109

were in the hall way and Scott decided to grab me by the throat and pin me up against the wall. Once he let go of me, I was out the door and off to work, with a brave face on. Once I arrived at work, it was show time. After that incident I promised myself I would never let him do that to me again.

I should have left.

Of course it happened again, and again. Pinning me up against the kitchen cupboards, throwing me out the front door, and chucking a cup of water over me in the morning whilst I was trying to get ready for work. It doesn't sound like much, but it was just another tactic to minimise me, making me feel worthless, while I had to wait to be let back in.

I had started to fight back. Every time he did try to pin me up I would full on punch him in the face. He didn't like that so much. It would get him off me. The whole situation was truly fucking horrible.

Of course, I know what you are thinking; why the fuck didn't I just get up and leave after the first time he did it? Never mind the second, third, fourth, fifth, blah, blah, blah.

The manipulator or the abuser will do a magnificent job at breaking you down. You just don't know whether you are coming or going. You believe that no one else will want you. You will feel worthless, ashamed, like it is all your fault. I blamed myself that he wasn't having sex. It was like I justified the behaviour because I wasn't putting out. All of it was my fault. I was to blame for everything. I didn't talk to anyone about it. There was so much shame. I was not about to start sharing what was really happening. I do not recognise the person I was when I was caught up with that situation. I had disappeared. The only control I had in all of it was my body. Had I given that away, I would have really disappeared. My soul would have been broken into million pieces.

I came across a leaflet at Fitness First. It was about a coach and athlete development course they were running at Bournemouth University, and I was looking for a new course to study. It was one night a week. I thought, 'How hard could it be?'

I applied, got an interview, and was accepted. I became a mature student at Bournemouth University in 2009. My first module was anatomy and physiology. On our first evening, the tutor introduced herself and then told us that we had a few minutes to put together a ten-minute presentation about energy systems. I shit myself and started panicking. My anxiety was through the roof. I grabbed a book. I couldn't see anything in it because I couldn't think straight. Of course, I knew it, but I was in such a state of panic I couldn't think about it. I thought, 'Right, I am good at delegating.' I told this guy in the class, who liked the sound of his own voice, that he was going to do all the talking, and I would just add stuff in. I basically blagged my way through the whole module.

Actually, I still have my very first assignment. I remember emailing my tutor warning her that it was bad. I did not have the first clue about construction, Harvard-style referencing, basically anything for that matter. She kindly emailed me back reassuring me that it would be fine.

Then I got an email from her, asking me to come and see her. I turned up at her office and she said, 'Janine, this essay!' Anyway, she passed me. We spoke a few years later about that essay and she shared that if she had failed me, I would have left and never looked back. She was one hundred percent right.

Being at university highlighted many insecurities that I thought I had dealt with. I'm not clever enough, or I'll never be good enough, would whirl around my brain. What the fuck am I

111

doing?

But I stuck with it. Ticked off each assignment and all I needed was a pass.

One evening I turned up and we were doing V02 max testing. I put myself forward to wear the mask. Don't ask why, my anxiety was always at an ultimate high in all my sessions. Before we could start the test, I had to take a resting heart rate. Usually, mine sits around 48 BPM. But that day, the test came out with 110. 'Holy fuck, Davis!' It is just as well that I was fit. It surprised me that no one questioned it. Not one person in the class asked why it was so high. We were studying the central nervous system, but as I have said, I was doing a pretty good job at covering up everything that was going on.

This one-day-a-week course at uni was meant to be part time, but for me there was no part time, about it. I was working full time, studying full time and training full time.

When I think about that time, I don't really know how I managed it all. I do know that it was my escape. Work, training and uni were my sanctuary, away from the bullshit I was going through at home.

I was now training for a world champs that was going to be held at the Bournemouth International Centre (BIC). I had to do the British Champs again to be able to qualify. I nailed that. British Champion, second time around. At the time, I was studying a particular module that was not so interesting. It was to do with health and safety at work, and financing. It was super dull. On the weekend of the competition, I had an assignment to produce and an exam to revise for. I did manage the assignment, but decided to blag the exam.

As I was entering the exam, my tutor asked how the comp went. I was surprised he knew about it. Fortunately for me, there had been a write up in the local newspaper with me in it. My tutor had been down the pub with his mates and spotted it.

When I sat to do the exam, I knew I was in trouble. I looked over the first page, and then the second, third, fourth, and fifth. I looked around the room and everyone was scribbling away, it was the worst feeling ever! I wasn't going to sit there and pretend like I knew what I was doing so I got up, walked over to my tutors desk, handed in my paper and left the room.

I was devastated! That was it, I had failed! I sobbed all the way home and as soon as I got back, I emailed my tutor to apologise profusely, and begged if I could do it again.

He went to the board, and fought my case. As I had been competing, I could take the exam again. I was super lucky that there were people at the Uni that wanted me to succeed.

Now my training was full throttle. I was squatting 180kg in kit, benching 105kg in a bench suit and deadlifting 185kg raw. At 75kg body weight, I was pushing some proper weight. The world champs was looming and I was hoping to get a 190kg squat. 110kg bench and get as close to 190kg deadlift as I could.

It was the day of the weigh-in and unlike my fighting career, where they would let 1kg go here and there, in powerlifting, you had to be on the money or under. If you were over you would not be able to lift. It was pretty stressful making weight but lucky for me it was a twenty-four-hour weigh-in. So, I could fast before weigh-in and then fill my boots with food once the weigh-in was done.

I was waiting outside the door of the weigh-in room and could see two men waiting with me. I thought to myself, 'Who are these guys?' and wondered what or who they were waiting for. At weigh-in you look around for your own competition, see who is going to be in your weight class.

It turns out that those *guys* were girls and had partaken in quite a lot of steroid consumption that now made them look very masculine to say the least. In fact, a lot of the women in the comp were all a little bit more on the side of taking steroids. I looked like the odd one out. But I didn't mind. Like I had said before, I knew where I was at. I knew who I was competing against. There were no cheats, as there are in the tested powerlifting organisations, no one hiding what they were doing.

One of the women I was competing against was from the US and she had a massive squat of 250kg. There was no way I was going to beat that. I just needed to stick to my game plan and concentrate on aiming for 190kg.

Squat was first, and I knew if I played everything right, I would walk away with silver. I managed all three lifts, the last being the 190kg squat. I was so happy! Next was the bench, and as I was busy warming up, I heard that the American woman who was beating me had to pull out due to injury. A big smile came over my face as I realised that I was then in contention of winning the world champs.

When I was lifting, Scott stayed well clear of me. I had sorted a couple of friends to help me prepare to go out. Knee wraps on, belt on tight, chalk on my back. One of my friends asked if I needed a slap around the face to gee me up. It told them that if they slapped me around the face, I would knock them the fuck out. You see all that behaviour in powerlifting and strongman events. They spend so much time at the side lines working themselves up, by the time they get out to do the lift they have nothing left. I did not need all that slapping and sniffing smelling salts bullshit; I just needed to focus and lift.

I achieved all three lifts with the bench press finishing with 110kg. The last three lifts are with the deadlift. I opened with

180kg. I went for 185kg next and then tried 187kg. I failed it, but that was OK, because I got my 185kg deadlift. I was sat down out the back of the stage and realised that I had done enough to be the world champion. Amazing! I couldn't believe it. I was now World Powerlifting Champion. So crazy.

Apparently, Scott had had enough. Scott wanted to go. Scott was bored. The day wasn't about Scott. I don't know why I just didn't say, 'NO.' I wasn't sure when I was getting my medal. I could see the stand going up for first, second and third places, but I just thought I would collect the following day. In most of the powerlifting competitions I had been too they would do all the lifting and give out all the medals at the end of the competition. Scott was so adamant about getting out of there I didn't have any time to ask when they were giving out the medals.

The day after competing I returned to the event. It turns out that I missed getting my medal, as they gave them out not long after I had finished competing. I was gutted! The organisers of the event disappeared for a moment and handed my medal to me there and then. Second time around at being a world champion and I didn't get to enjoy receiving it in front of everyone that had come along to support me. There is something really special about being on the podium and achieving what you have achieved, along with everyone stood there clapping for you and cheering for your acceptance of winning the world title.

Of all the things Scott had done to me, that one sits up there in the top five of shitbag things.

It didn't matter though; I was now a world champion powerlifter!

A week after the powerlifting champs, a friend of mine had signed me up to a race called 'The Grim'. It was an eight-mile run across a tank course. I had done zip training for it. It was the parallel opposite of the lifting, but, in for a penny, in for a pound. All I had to do was finish it. Time didn't matter. I started, ran the eight miles and finished it. Job done. You put your mind to anything, and you can generally get the job done.

Just a word of advice: I do not recommend anyone running eight miles if you have not trained for it. At that time I was cycling everywhere. My cardio was fit enough and I had my back ground in fighting. I knew that my mental strength would get me through it.

Vodka Is King

I finished my foundation degree and passed it by the skin of my teeth. You had to achieve a certain percentage to be accepted on to the sports psychology degree. I wasn't sure that the tutors on my foundation course were going to let me step up to do the BSc. I did know that I hadn't achieved the percentage to move on.

My rational mind tells me I'm not stupid, but there is that little voice in my head *'You're not good enough'*. I was always so far behind the rest of my peers in understanding how to write and format essays. I felt I was blagging it all the way. The careers advisor back when I was fifteen would pop up in my mind and keep reiterating, 'You are not clever enough.' I was no good. I did not belong. I certainly never told anyone this, but I was like a duck on water. I was gliding my way through academic life, looking like I had my shit together, but really on the inside I was a complete mess. My consciousness was pushing hard against the tide, but I always felt I was getting nowhere.

My graduation for my foundation degree was fun! I got to wear the cap and gown. My name was called and I walked across the stage to receive my certificate. I had completed it and achieved my degree in coach and athlete development against all the odds of thinking that I could not do it. I showed myself that I could do it.

Fortunately, the tutors of the University who made the decisions of who would continue on to the BSc, decided to give me the opportunity to participate. Whilst I didn't think I was good enough to be there, I was not about to give in. It is better to try and fail than to not try at all!

Scott's behaviour was atrocious, bordering on torturous. For him, any attention was better than no attention. He was happy whenever he got a response out of me, in any context. Meaning, if I was out of control with rage because he had sat there for thirty minutes repeating, 'Davis, Davis, Davis, Davis, Davis, Davis, Davis, Davis, Davis, Davis, Davis, Davis, Davis, Davis, Davis, Davis,' he was happy. What a twisted individual.

After I had lost my shit, he would then say, 'Look at you, look at the state of you!'

I asked once, 'Why? Why do you do it?' He would have a sadistic smile on his face, and say nothing in response.

I could have given him everything. Everything of myself emotionally and financially. It would never have been enough. From what I understand, a narcissist takes great pleasure in seeking out a strong individual and breaking them down. I didn't give him everything though, did I? The one thing I kept for myself was my body. I would not give that up!

I did not want him touching me. I just couldn't do it. His behaviour towards me was so sickening that the last thing I wanted was to have sex with him. I know that drove him mad. I was strong enough to hold on to that one thing of myself. He could never see that if he had just been a better person, I would have let him in. As I have said before, his response always was to ask if I was a lesbian. That amused me. Such a dick. I justified his behaviour because I was not putting out. I suppose that was one of the reasons I stayed as long as I did. It is all about the shame and embarrassment because I was not giving him sex. So, I deserved right? It must be all my fault, right?

This is what a manipulator does. Chips away at your self-esteem. Makes you think that you are the problem in your relationship. Makes you believe that no one else is going to want you.

He would actually say that to me, 'Who the fuck is going to want you?' Unfortunately, when you hear it enough, you start to believe it.

I hated him, but I didn't know how to get rid of him. I didn't have a way out.

I started to confide in my mum. I don't know why. I'm such a twat. I just wanted her to be my mum. Her response was that she did not want me turning up on her doorstep!

Trust me, although I was caught up in that shit with him, and I wanted out of there, I would rather stay with the monster than move back in that house with the devil.

My mum is charming and pleasant to be around to start with; you think that things are going to be OK, that this time it will be different.

As usual, it doesn't take long for the bullshit to start all over again.

Mum was around my flat one night, talking about Leigh being abused as a boy while he spent time with my dad. It was exhausting spending time with her. It was all bullshit. I told her it was none of her business and that if it had happened, it was Leigh's business and she was to leave him alone. This went on for three hours. Fuck! I could not wait to get her out of the house.

I'm not sure what kind of behavioural disorder a person has where they construct falsified stories, and then live them as if they truly happened.

The next story she came up with was having sex with a co-worker, who was a truck driver like herself. He apparently filmed them having sex in the back of truck where the drivers sleep and

119

put the film on a website without her knowledge. She went as far as saying she had the police turn up and everything. It was all very strange. I couldn't get my head around it. I mean, I know camera phones have progressed massively in the last ten years, but this was 2009-ish. The phone needed to be really big to film them both. Have you seen the cab of a truck? It's pretty small. Where would he have hidden it? I started asking questions, but she always had an answer for what had happened; it was all very weird. I never saw the police turn up at her house, nor was I ever present when the police turned up. I just sat there looking at her and thinking, 'You are a nut job.'

I believed her at first, of course. I am a gullible twat and want to see the good in everyone. She was my mum! I didn't like to think that someone had done that to her. I had even told some of my tough guy friends. I was putting together a crew to go sort this guy out. But then I started thinking about the whole situation. It was just not adding up. The cameras on the phones then would just not have been good enough to get a complete picture of who she was. Why go to such lengths? It's just fucking crazy!

Scott took to ripping my books up. I liked to go to bed early and read. He would come in to the bedroom because he wanted attention, and, if I did not give him what he wanted, he would take my books and rip them in half. I knew he was talking to prostitutes, along with most of my friends on my phone. Most of my true mates would ignore him and tell him to fuck off. But I had this client at the time and she kept cancelling on me. I would turn up for the sessions, she would appear and pay me the full amount and then leave. I didn't think anything about it at the time. Until, I was at home one day and Scott had left his phone. I would quite often go through it, because I knew he was up to all kinds of shit, and I was curious. I found explicit sexual messages on there. They went on and on and on about what she was going to do to him. What he was going to do to her. Again, I justified it because it was my fault. Of course he was going to go elsewhere. I was to blame for his behaviour. I typed the number into my phone. It was my client that kept cancelling on me. What the fuck!

Not long before this, I had a dream. If they are really vivid, I will look up the meaning. I don't know how these people on Google know how to interpret dreams, but it is something that I do to try and make sense of what they mean. The interpretation was that someone close to me was deceiving me. Hmm, who could that be?

I knew there was a woman at The Bulldog causing problems for me. She was shit-stirring. She was a bully too. Whenever you sparred her, you would just be getting into a flow, and she would start moaning about how hard you were going on her. I would take it easy, pull my power down to forty percent. She would then seize her opportunity whilst you were taking your foot off the gas and clump you really hard in the head. There were numerous occasions when I threw her out of the ring for doing that. Just bullshit behaviour. She was happy to bully the beginners and tell the new students in the beginners' sessions how hard she was. I had heard of this carry-on and decided to turn up to the advanced fighters' session. All the women there hated me. They would be out the back in the changing rooms all talking shit about me and then be nice to my face. I had found out that they would say, 'I hope Janine is not coming tonight.' Stupid twats. I sparred with the instigator of the bullshit and really decided to put it on her a bit. I wasn't going to give her any opportunity to bail out. I really pushed her to her limits. Dave was there. She was desperate to be a coach, so she didn't want to lose face. She had to take what was

121

being given.

We were talking a couple of days after that. She had told me that she ended up down the hospital with a tear, I think in her stomach or somewhere round that region, due to a kick that I had given her. This is contact sport. What happens in the gym stays in the gym. The damage was not purposeful, it is just what happens sometimes. I went there that night just to make a point and put her in her place.

On my visit with Dave not long after this incident, he mentioned that I was a bit tough on her. I shrugged my shoulders. I thought he was going soft. I started to think about the number of beatings he had put me through. But apparently, I was being tough on her. Fuck you, Dave.

So naturally, I assumed the dream was about her, because of all the backstabbing going on in the gym.

I then realised, when I found the text messages, that it was my client. I messaged her there and then! I told her, 'I knew.' She wanted to meet. I said, 'NO WAY!' Everyone assumes that I am going to beat them up, but I am smarter than that. Indifference is far better. She wanted me to hit her, because then she could play the victim in what she had done. I told her that we would never be friends again. I was not about to waste my time talking to her. As for him, I also included that my time would come to be rid of that asshole.

I confronted him about it, but I didn't leave. I'm the fucking asshole for staying. He would brush it off and say it was all a joke, that he didn't mean it. He would say that all the time.

I asked him, 'Why do you tell them that you love them?'

'I'm just messing around; I don't really mean it.'

There were occasions where I would try to run away and every time I did, he frequently chased me down the road.

122

Back to university. Get my head back into my studies. My anxiety and panic attacks were pretty bad around then. I never really had an attack, but the thought of having one was always at the brink of my everyday thoughts. I always ensured I had the seat by the door, I did not want to be trapped at the back of the room in the corner with all the twenty-year-olds surrounding me. I needed to make sure there was an escape so that, if an episode happened, no one knew. I kept all of that suffering to myself. I found my coping strategies and I got on with surviving day to day.

I was doing all right with the BSc. I was passing my modules, but, one of my sports psychology lecturers was super lazy with teaching. I was so caught up with my insecurities I did not challenger her. Her lessons consisted of:

Bring a journal, stand up in front of everyone.

Read it out.

Discuss.

Copy a PowerPoint presentation.

EVERY SESSION. It was so boring! Most of the journals I did not understand. I was in a class full of twenty-something year olds! I felt really stupid because I didn't understand the journals. So, I stopped going. To be honest, I know everyone stopped going. On reflection now, I know that I should have asked questions and not worried about what anyone thought of me. I was paying to be taught. There was no teaching going on in that session at all. Copy and paste, week after week. The same delivery of teaching was the method of delivering her sessions.

I went to see her towards the end of the course. I tried to open up about what I was going through and how much I was struggling. I just wanted some empathy and compassion. Unfortunately, despite this woman being a psychology lecturer and practitioner, she had nothing for me. I told her that I wanted to pursue a master's, she told me that I would not be able to do it.

I looked at her and thought, 'Fuck you!' Just another fucking dick telling me that I was not capable. That was the last time we properly spoke. I got my head down at uni and just decided to keep moving forwards the best way I knew how.

At home with Scott was just a continuous minefield of him drinking copious amounts of vodka. The cars that we went through were unbelievable. He couldn't look after anything. In the eleven years we were together, we went through thirteen cars! THIRTEEN. If he just earned a bit more money and decided to get off his lazy ass and do more work, our life just would've been a bit more comfortable. But really, that wasn't part of his plan. I was there to subsidise his lifestyle. Why work when he's got me to pay for everything?

On one occasion, we had a lovely Rover. A really nice car, but the head gasket had gone. We tried to fix it ourselves. Of course, everyone has an opinion. We had at least three of his mates who are not mechanics telling him how to fix it! It would have been nice to take it to the garage and have it fixed properly. Lacking the money to do that, it sat outside our flat in the road until he decided what we were going to do with it. He then purchased another shit car, another Rover. But this Rover was a different model to the one that had stopped working.

Scott was a fairly intelligent person but, his common sense was unbelievably stupid. Off-the-scale stupid. It would astound me, the stupidity of the things he would suggest, and ultimately, try to do.

Scott decided he liked the wheels on the Rover that had broken down. He announced that he was going to take the wheels off that car and put it on the Rover that was working.

I said, 'It won't work, they are different models. The wheels will not fit!'

He insisted, 'I like those wheels, I am going to put them on the Rover that is working.'

'It won't work, they are different models.'

His response was to shout at me like I didn't know what I was talking about and proceeded to start taking the wheels off the Rover that was not working.

I thought, 'Great he'll be out of my hair for at least a few hours.' I went up to the flat and pottered around in peace. Until he came into the flat and said, 'The wheels don't fit!'

'No shit!'

This is what Scott decided to do.

Instead of putting the wheels back where he got them from, he decided to pile them up in the communal hallway of the flats. Leave the Rover in the street with no wheels on it and just fuck off out.

In the morning, I woke up to police aware stickers all over the car, because it is illegal to have a car in the road that is not road-worthy, and a note in the hallway from the residents of the block telling us to remove the tyres. Rightly so, of course.

Another car we owned had a radiator problem. Every time we went somewhere, we had to carry litre bottles of water to fill it up. Again, it would have been nice just to go and get it fixed! But, no. We had to carry bottles of water to fill up the car everywhere we went. Scott picked me up from coaching one night. He was in the process of filling up the car with water. He walks back into the gym and says,' You never guess what I have done?'

I looked at him with disdain and said, 'What the fuck now?'

His proud response: 'I have put the water in the petrol tank.'

'What the actual fuck! Why would you put water in the petrol tank?' He opened up the petrol cap and emptied a two-litre bottle of water into the petrol tank. Honestly, the despair that I would feel was not measurable on most days.

He didn't give a fuck, because it was me paying for it all.

We managed to get half-way across town before the car died. I lost my shit and steamed off down the road and told him that he needed to fucking fix it!

I was still cycling everywhere; it was winter time and the temperature was below freezing. The gym I was teaching in had no heating, it was minus two even inside. When I'm coaching, I am not moving around as much as my students. If you have back-to-back clients you can get really cold. By the time I would finish coaching I was already in pain from being in freezing conditions. My legs were numb trying to cycling home. It was like they just wanted to shut down; it was exhausting and soul destroying.

If I couldn't bear cycling in the morning, I would get him to drop me off. One morning, I sat in the passenger's side of the car. I thought something looked wrong. It was pouring with rain and the windshields didn't look right. I then figured out that the car only had one windshield wiper, and it was on my side. The driver's side wiper had been snapped off.

I never understand that behaviour from someone just walking down the street. Why would someone do that? I stated, 'We've only got one windshield wiper.'

Scott knew and just didn't say anything because he knew I would kick up a fuss. It was dangerous, and if the police saw him, he'd get pulled over and that would be a fine of some sort that I would have to pay.

Scott told me, 'Be quiet,' as he continued driving and was

126

trying to look out the windscreen of the passenger's side so that he could see. I could not wait to get out of the car. I said, 'Get it fucking sorted!'

I was always made out to be the aggressor in our relationship. Scott would always refer to me as The Terminator. Everyone would laugh and think I was the asshole, but little did they know the chaos and constant stress I was living in.

Birthdays, anniversaries, Christmas, were non-events really. He would just not bother to do anything. I gave up a lot of the time telling him when my birthday was. For years he didn't bother. One year I told him that he was going to get me a Christmas gift. I even gave him some money for it. He asked me what I wanted. I said, 'No, you go and think about what I might like.'

He came back with a box. I opened this box on Christmas morning. Now, we lived in an attic flat. Yes, it had no garden! I opened the box and pulled out a garden ornament. A solar-powered garden ornament. I looked at it. I politely said, 'Thank you,' and stuck it in the corner of our attic flat. He bought it because he liked the cherubs on it.

After the Christmas present fiasco, I told him the same thing for my birthday. This year he would do something for me. Again, he said, 'What do you want?'

'No, you think about it.'

Really, I was asking for trouble!

He wanted a party. It was a great party. All my friends were there. We had a great time. My brother decided to put in a karaoke machine. God knows why. Me and Leigh had NEVER done karaoke before! Leigh's choice of song for both of us to do was, Shakira's 'Your Hips Don't Lie'. It was hilarious! Definitely a moment in time where you need to be there to understand how hilarious it was. Me and him singing, both of us tone deaf.

But the party was for Scott. Not for me. A great excuse to get completely wankered.

It took him eleven years to actually figure out how to buy me something that I wanted. (spoiler alert) On our last Christmas together, he bought me a (sorry, correction, his mum bought me) a laptop to study on and a North Face gilet. Eleven years to figure that one out. Too little, too late by that time.

Scott's mum was an enabler to his behaviour really. Scott had never learnt the word 'No.' She just gave him whatever he wanted. He asked for money, she said yes; he asked basically for anything, and she always said yes. He didn't really understand the value in anything, because his mum was always there to pick up the pieces. He never had to take account for any of his behaviour because Mummy always bailed him out.

I would say 'No' all the time. I would always bring his behaviour up and try to get him to do better. To be better. To stop lying. To try to be honest. But it was a waste of time really. I was just a surrogate mum in that relationship. I had a man baby to look after.

I was cycling home from uni one day and my old powerlifting coach saw me. He pulled over and asked me to come back to training, to start Olympic lifting. I was thirty-six at this point and I thought 'Yeah, this will be good. Give me another direction to go in.'

It wasn't long after being back and training with him that we were competing again. The first competition was the English champs at senior level. I went and conquered; I became an English weightlifting champ! The next was the British Masters in Olympic lifting. Yes, you guessed it I got my very first British Championship at Masters level.

After my interlude with the psychology lecturer, I was really starting to struggle with university. I was going to jack it all in because I just felt that I wasn't getting it. Everyone around me seemed to understand it all and I felt completely out of my depth. But there was a tutor there. That was my very first tutor I had. Kelly. She was the tutor that had passed my very first assignment (That really should have had a 'Fail' on it). I emailed her and told her that I was not coming back. The pressure of full-time work and full-time study was too much. Also, I still don't get academia to this day. My brain is not academic-minded. I could see all the youngsters around me, busy writing and understanding it all while I'm just thinking about how I'm fucking stupid and wondering what the fuck was I doing there any-way.

Kelly emailed me back straight away. She demanded that I come and see her first thing to talk it through before I made any final decisions. In fact, if I remember rightly, she called me that day at home. We had a good chat and she talked me into staying. She said,' You have come this far, do not give up now!'

She was right, of course. I finished my degree. I didn't get a First but, little old me that had left school twenty years before that with nothing, and was told that I was stupid by that ridiculous careers advisor, got my BSc in Sports Psychology and Physiology. Me, an academic!

This graduation I didn't get to go to. I didn't have enough money for the cap and gown. That motherfucker Scott was too engrossed in making his first film, which I was subsidising.

Scott's dad's health was deteriorating. His heart was a mess. He kept having repeated heart attacks. Scott's mum was bearing the brunt of caring for him. I had suggested at Christmas that I would take care of cooking Christmas dinner. It was just too much for Scott's mum in the end. The first Christmas was fine. It was just the four of us. It was lovely and quiet and a great help to Scott's mum. Leigh came one year. That was nice. Just to have someone there that was on my side. I also invited Mum one year. I told her dinner would be at three p.m.

If I say dinner is going to be at three, it will be at three. I had dinner ready at three! Everything was fresh and ready to serve at three! No Mum. Ten past three, no Mum. Everyone is now waiting for her to arrive. Twenty past three, still no Mum. Dinner is now getting cold and I'm pissed at the fact we were waiting for her to turn up. I mean, what the fuck? I can forgive ten minutes, but she eventually turned up at three thirty, only to blame me for being on time. Her words, 'Trust you to be ready at three.'

I just looked at her. No sorry, no explanation. It was all my fault. Mum sat down at the dinner table and started bringing up stories about me and Leigh when we were kids and how awful we were. She would never take responsibility for her own behaviour or even for a minute talk about how awful she was. I would always fall back into abusive parent, submissive child mode. When I think about it, it makes me cross. I would never say anything. I would never challenge her on it. I would revert straight back to the control that abusive parent has and just let her do it. She never, ever took responsibility for her behaviour; it was always someone else's fault.

The following Christmas dinners turned into an absolute fiasco of me cooking for the whole of Scott's family, meeting their demands of what they liked and didn't like. I mean, all they had to do was turn up and eat. I always thought it was cheeky. Not grateful at all that it was me doing the dinner and the hard graft.

I will say though, that if I am in the kitchen cooking, I have figured out in my head how it is all planned out. What I do not like is people coming in and messing with my system. Control freak or just a master at my game, call it what you want. If I'm doing it, I'm doing it my way, without interruption. Of course, Scott would never get involved in helping. Scott's mum would like to be in the kitchen doing something. I always felt like she judged me. I knew she didn't like how I pushed Scott to try to be better. All I wanted was to be left in the kitchen to just get on with it!

Machine Martial Arts was still cruising along nicely. I always had students turning up to the session which meant a fresh supply of new meat to train. Unfortunately for me, as a woman who teaches martial arts, you get the odd man either trying to test you or even take over for you. I had one man turn up and inform me that he was going to help me teach the session!

He did not ask if I wanted help, he TOLD ME he was going to help me. Cheeky fuck! I had a Latvian man turn up to my session on another occasion. He opened the door to the studio and snaked his way around the class to the back. Peering out of his eyes at me and what I was teaching. To be honest, I have never had much respect from the Eastern Europeans when I have been teaching Thai boxing. They either do not acknowledge that I exist or they try to beat me up. I thought, 'What does this motherfucker want?'

He informed me that he will come to the next session. I agreed and thought I would just play it by ear. If he plays up, I will fuck him off. For the most part, he was good as gold but, on one occasion though, I used him as a dummy to demonstrate the next skill the class would be learning. I had three men stood by, watching me teach. As I started to demonstrate the skill, the Latvian started to fight me. He was trying to get the better of me in front of the men. Well, I had two choices: I let him win, or fucking sort the situation out. I was demonstrating a stand-up wrestling move. It's called clinch work in Thai boxing. As the Latvian was trying to fight me, I somehow managed to jump up and wedge my knees into his hips, position my arms around his neck, and jump down onto my feet and choke him. This was not a move in clinch work. This was a move to shut him the fuck down. I held onto it just a bit longer than I needed to. Just so that I could hear him gagging a little bit.

One of the men watching, Paul, was clapping his hands. 'Yes, Janine. Guillotine choke hold, brilliant.'

I let go of the Latvian, and looked at him, I didn't need to say anything other than, 'Shall we start again?'

Fucking dick!

At the beginning of the session, if anyone new turned up, I would make a point of introducing myself and just get some background information from them. This one dude turned up one night. I went to shake hands with him and, as he shook my hand, he squeezed my fingers. My instant reaction was 'Fucking dick!' Who does that? I'll tell you who does that. Fucking idiots with teeny weeny little dicks. Men that have got something to prove! 'Right,' I thought, 'here we go.'

I set the session up. We were to work on defence this particular night. Punch defence and kick defence. I got everyone partnered up and we were to take it in turns. The whole idea is to learn without being beaten up. Use about sixty percent of your power. Learn to take contact without having to survive.

This dude kept finding his way back to me. I set straight arm punch defence and hook defence. Instead of working those punches, he would add uppercuts and obscure punches, trying to catch me out. I stayed calm, kept bringing him back to what the session was. When it was kicking defence, he was doing all kinds of different kicks that were outside of what I was teaching. He was being a little prick. Again, I stayed calm, told him those kicks are not part of the skill we were working. He did not want to listen though. I then thought, 'Fuck you, let's have it.' It was the end of the session. I had just about had enough of him; he kept punching me in the face. I could have taken the high road and told him that this session is not for him. Instead, I decided to beat him up and down the studio with one glove on, because my other glove had fallen off whilst I was trying to hit him. Pretty much the whole session stopped what they were doing to watch me give this little shit a hiding. He came back for one session to save face. I never saw him again after that.

I would run a sparring session at the end of the week for some of the students that were interested in fighting. One of these nights, I decided to join in. I had said to the students (who were all men) this particular evening that I would spar with them technically, which means light power. I could pick them up on their openings and show them where they were making mistakes. The session was going fine, except for this one lad, who was a child really. He was sixteen or seventeen, but he was six foot one! He was pretty tall to my five-foot-eight height. From what I understood, he was a bit of a bully at school because he was bigger than everyone else. He was used to throwing his weight around. He never showed that behaviour in my sessions, but I did have grown men in my sessions that would have put him right in his place. Let's call him Joe.

Joe found his way round to me, 'Me and you, Janine.'

'Sure, Joe.'

Joe stipulated boxing only. 'No problem, Joe.'

I always insisted that the younger guys wore head guards, at least until they were eighteen. The round started. The first shot he threw came in, massive and out of nowhere, and clumped me round the head. I thought, 'What the fuck is he doing?' I had already said light contact. I didn't respond. He threw another shot. Clumped me again round the head. Now, I realised he was trying to prove something. Another clump came in and then another. This cheeky little big shit was trying to knock me out. Right, game on. Sorry people, I know he was young but this little motherfucker needed to be put back inside his young tall box and learn some respect.

I hit him as hard as I could for the rest of the round. We had an all-out war. I didn't knock him out. That wasn't my intention. He just needed to know that I had the goods to give back. The bell went. I was fuming. He took his head guard off and threw it across the ring and loped off to the toilets to sulk. I continued with the session like nothing had happened. When he decided to re-appear, he was rubbing his thumb. I asked him, 'What's the problem?'

'I've hurt my thumb!'

'Well, you should not have been hitting me so hard in the head.'

I then also told him that if he wanted to learn I could teach him, but if he wanted a war, I could do that as well. He sheepishly rubbed his thumb and couldn't look me in the eye. I told him to go and get on the bag. He never came back to my sessions. I know that he went and joined a martial arts club that had no problem throwing people into fights with no training. I hadn't put him off the sport, he just had to find somewhere else to feed his ego.

Scott was fighting a fair amount around this time. He was doing all right. He was super strong so that always gave him an advantage. Dave from The Bulldog was regularly putting on fight shows in Bournemouth and he was looking for a heavyweight.

Dave asked if Scott would fight one of his guys on one of his shows. Dave thought his guy was better than Scott. Dave's guy was a heavyweight, but not through muscle. He was just a fat lump.

People that have never done weights properly underestimate the difference between someone who does weights and someone who doesn't. I always found that when I was fighting, my strength always gave me an advantage. Scott's strength was powerful. He could deadlift 300kg and squat 300kg. Getting clumped in the face by someone that strong is not a joke.

Dave was being weird on the day of the fight. One minute he was in the corner, the next he was saying it's going to be weird because I was in the opposite corner. I just ignored him and got on with what I needed to and that was to make sure that Scott was ready to go out and fight. Dave ended up in the corner. Scott forgot to put his groin guard on. The referee, before the fight starts, will ask to see the gumshield and ask the men if they are wearing a groin guard. Scott said 'Yes,' knowing full well he had forgotten to put it on.

The ref then tapped his dick, looked at him and said, 'go and put it on!'

Scott ran to the warm up room. I met him there. I saw the look of panic and doubt on his face. I told him to pull his shit together and put the fucking guard on and get back out there and fight!

The bell went. Dave's guy was putting up a good enough start. Scott had him up against the ropes and puts in this uppercut, Ooh, you hear the crunch on the guy's forehead. He looks up and he is bleeding. The ref stops the fight for the doc to look at it. The next thing you know is that the ref has stopped the fight. It's over. I had seen Dave's guy talking to the doc in the ring. The doc had asked him if he wanted to carry on. Dave's guy said no, he wanted out. I mean, who could blame him? I wouldn't want to be in there with Scott, being clumped round the head.

The following day in the fight shop, I was talking with Dave. He was blah, blahing shit about the fight and the doctor stopping it. I said, 'No, your guy gave up!'

Dave tried to argue the toss with me. Then he said, 'I've got the fight night here, let's watch it.'

You could blatantly see Dave's guy talking to the doc and the doc asking him if he wanted to continue. Dave's guy says no, and gives up. Fuck you, Dave, you don't know shit. That shut him up quick smart!

Scott was pretty focused when he was training for his fights. He probably was still drinking, who knows. I was always super happy when he was out on the weekends and I could spend some time on my own at the flat. We generally never went out together. I was sober; he was drinking, taking drugs, and getting shit-faced. I just didn't want to be around it.

His moods would change from one day to the next. Either because he was taking steroids or on a come down from whatever he had been doing the night before. I got home one day from doing my PT sessions and he was on one of his kick-off moods. I knew straight away. I was trying to keep my cool and keep the interaction balanced and cool. I had my next session to get to, which was at a school.

Local schools would employ me to go in and teach martial arts to the kids as an after-school activity.

By the time we made it into the car, the interaction between us was getting prickly and I was not holding my shit together. We had literally got to the end of the road to a junction and we were now screaming at each other. I was driving through Southbourne, a little suburb of Bournemouth, in the daytime, with Scott's hand round my throat trying to strangle me. How I didn't end up crashing is beyond me. I held on to the steering wheel while I was trying to get my breath. He let go and I turned left down this road. I then back fisted him straight in the face. Split his lip open and was screaming for him to get out of the car!

He wouldn't get out, he wouldn't leave. In the back of my head, I was thinking, 'I am going to be late for my kids' session. I do not want to let them down.' He wouldn't get out of the car. So, I carried on driving until I reached the school, got out of the car and got into the session with the kids like it was show time and nothing had just happened.

Do you know how hard that is to do?

Yes, I know. Why didn't I just leave?

I was on my own trying to find my way out of the bullshit I was caught up in. Do you know how many times that mother-fucker apologised, and how many times I thought, 'Maybe this time he will be better.'

I always used to say about women caught up in abusive relationships. JUST LEAVE. Why don't you just leave? Let me tell you something: it is not that easy.

I ask myself about the good times. Yes, we would laugh, we could talk about all kinds of different shit. There were moments after his really bad behaviour that he would leave letters. He would promise to be better and he would (for a moment) say how much he loved me. Of course, that would last a mere couple of weeks. I would always give him the benefit of the doubt. I would think there was maybe a ray of light in him being better, all for that to diminish. I would go back to hating him and trying to survive.

Scott's behaviour was so erratic that it would be difficult to

137

tell you how much he was drinking. He could have been drinking every day. I just didn't know. His day would consist of working just the mornings because that was all he could manage. Then he'd be passed out on the couch for most of the days recovering from the drinking and drug taking.

I would find the hidden vodka bottles around the flat. The worst would be when we would go out together with friends and he would try to disguise it in either a Ribena bottle or a Lucozade bottle. I would watch him across the dinner table and think, 'You are a fucking asshole.' I knew what he was doing and he thought that no one else knew. I FUCKING KNEW! The joke of it was that he would end up with Ribena marks like a five-year-old at the corners of his mouth.

We were invited to an afternoon lunch at a friend's. I knew what he was up to. I could see him trying to hide the vodka bottle down the front of his pants. He was walking weird because otherwise the vodka bottle would fall down his trousers.

Deceit is the worst, the lies and then abusive behaviour. One year rolled into another year, into another year. The years just seemed to slip away from me. Every year I would think the same. 'How the fuck do I get out of this?'

Living with him in the house and his own chaos meant I was living with his untidiness. He never cleaned. He never did anything to be fair. If I said about him even cooking dinner once in a while, he would say that I was really fussy. I do like what I like. It's not that difficult to prepare something for me. Chicken, vegetables and rice. That's pretty straight forward. But his response would be, 'Well you don't like chips, eggs and sausages.'

No, I do not want chips, eggs and sausages! I mean, we'd been together long enough for him to know what the fuck I like.

I made spicy meatballs. I like that dish. I would make it with a pre-made spicy mix. He liked it as well. One evening that I made it, I didn't have the usual mix. I used a piri-piri mix. I used half the bottle. Oh my god, it was fucking hot. Now, I don't mind spice and I don't mind it being really hot. Even I said to myself how hot it was. I told him when he came in. He replied, 'I'm sure it will be fine.'

I knew full well that he was going to hate it because his level of hot is a korma at an Indian. I sat back and watched him take a mouthful. It wasn't in his mouth more than a second before he spat it out and told me how disgusting it was. I laughed, oh my god I laughed. His pain was my joy.

Another time I had made an apple crumble. I make a good apple crumble. He loved my apple crumble. He had been looking forward to it all day. I had decided to use wholewheat flour instead of the white flour that I usually used. I just thought I'd try it to see how it turns out. I served it up and was in the kitchen when I heard this voice bellowing from the lounge.

'What the fuck have you done? It's fucking different!'

'I used a different flour.'

'Well, fucking don't. It doesn't taste right!'

I went back in the kitchen and laughed at that as well, stupid twat.

OK, maybe his lack of tidying was an exaggeration. He did sort of clean, maybe once and while. He certainly pulled his weight a bit after I had lost my shit a few times.

However, there was this one time that I had come home from teaching. It was a Friday and I had been to the shops to get myself some treats, knowing full well that he was going to be out. I was so excited; I could watch what I wanted on the TV. Sit on the couch without having him fucking laying his eighteen stone body all over me, demanding that I rub his head.

I could sit, eat my treats and have a lovely time. God knows where he was. I didn't care.

After I had finished some of my treats, I looked down on the couch where his duvet was and saw a nugget of something. 'What the fuck is that!'

On closer inspection, it was a golf ball-sized piece of shit!

I was more annoyed by that fact that I had just eaten my treats while sitting in his shit. I brought it up with him the following day.

'So, you are now just shitting on the sofa?'

He just laughed. He thought it was hilarious.

This is a guy that wanted me to have sex with him. But, of course, it was all my doing. I'm the lesbian, I'm the asexual. Of course, he would never think that, just maybe, it was down to how he was treating me and behaving around the house.

Scott's quote to get me into bed was, 'I don't know what all the fuss is about, all you've got to do is open your legs! Just lay back and open your legs!'

I just found the whole thing so disgusting.

Men, let me tell you something. If your partner is not having sex with you, take a look at how you are treating them. That will generally be the cause as to why they do not want you to touch them.

There has to be an attraction and you have got to woo us; make us feel special, and not just like an object that you want to fuck!

Well, that's how I feel anyway.

I received a message from Cassandra, who married Rafael's friend Jose back in the '90s. As a recap, I had completely fallen in love with Rafael back in the '90s and held on to my love addiction towards him. Jose was an asshole to Cassandra. You don't need to know the details, but trust me. He was just a selfish prick. Cassandra had left him quite a few years before and he was reaching out to say that he had changed. She of course said, 'Fuck that shit, I do not want him all up in my business!'

Cassandra had forwarded the email that Jose had sent to her. I thought, 'Ooh, I wonder if he is still in touch with Rafael?'

I sat in front of my computer on many occasions to email him to ask Jose about Rafael, but I felt like I was cheating. It didn't matter that I knew Scott was talking to prostitutes, or telling women on Facebook that he loved them. I also started to find video clips of him filming his penis. Was he just watching himself, or sending them out to women? He can't be that much of a narcissist that he's filming his own dick and watching it back.

I just couldn't send the email. I couldn't behave that way. I had too much respect for myself. I tucked that contact away until I was in a position to use it. Rafael was never too far away from my thoughts. I didn't think about him all the time, but he would surface. I would think about our time together, and how much I missed him.

Scott was drinking heavily at this point. The drugs were pretty prolific as well: coke, MDMA, GHB, and steroids. His behaviour was just truly awful. I had never been afraid of him. I was always able to fight back. Stand up for myself. But one night, it went too far. He grabbed the back of my head, pushed me down to the sofa and buried my head into the cushions. He held it down just long enough for me not to be able to breathe. It was the first time that I was scared for my life.

I immediately left the living room and went to bed. Scott stayed in the living room. I knew I needed help. I took myself off to the doctors. I thought that maybe they could point me in the direction of me being able to help him. I wasn't even looking for help myself. I thought that maybe someone would be able to help me help him.

The doctor basically berated me for twenty minutes. She told me it was all my fault and that I should leave him. She told me that he would ruin me. I was the reason for his drinking. Eventually, she give me a number for a support group. I left there feeling like absolute shit. If I was any less of a person I would have gone home and topped myself. But I thought, 'Fuck her, what a fucking bitch.'

The next occasion that I went to the doctor's, which wasn't long after I had seen the bitch doctor, I could see the notes on the screen when I was in the room with the doctor. She wrote that I was desperate and needed help. I mean, what the actual fuck! I was asking for help and I got nothing.

I did seek out the support group. It was called The Butterfly Project. I phoned them and went along to see what it was all about. It was weird. I walked into the space where these two people were sat opposite each other across these massive tables. They looked at me, said nothing. I sat down, assuming that one of them would maybe talk to me or take me to a room where we could talk.

Nope, we just sat there saying nothing. 'Right, fuck this', I thought, 'I'm going to start talking.' I just started to open up. They listened. They were empathetic, gave me some leaflets to recognise the abuser and then offered that I join an abused women's circle group.

I left thinking I did not want to join a group. It was just not my thing. People annoy me, those types of groups annoy me. I just needed to figure out what I was going to do next. I didn't go back.

The doctor had reported it to the police. I had a phone call from an officer asking me if I wanted to press charges. I said, 'No.'

I had started looking at flats to move into. I had also confided in my mum. Why? I don't know. I just needed someone to be on my side. She had already told me that she didn't want me turning up on her doorstep. I was now confiding in her about Scott's behaviour and how I was earning great money and wasn't able to enjoy that fact because that lazy fuck did not want to work. I had started to secretly move some of my stuff out. I thought if I could get the chunk of it out. I could do a clean sweep whilst he was out and do a bunk without him knowing. I asked Mum if I could store some of it at her place. She agreed. I took all my dress shoes, around twenty pairs of shoes and my roller boots and stored them in one of her rooms that she wasn't using. All she had in that room was stuff she had collected from the dump.

Mum phoned me one day and said, 'Let's go to the shops, hang out.'

I thought, 'Yeah, cool. Give me a break from the house.'

We were having a lovely afternoon, I thought. We were really making some headway in our relationship. We were actually having a nice time. It made me feel good for a change. It wasn't hard work. We then pulled up outside my flat. This was when the ambush started. She started in with, 'What are you going to do?'

I don't even know if she was doing it for my own good. It went on for an hour. She was slowly but surely trying to break me down. I know the feeling that I felt was heavy. I knew I had to leave him. But leaving an abuser is never as easy as just walking out the door. What I didn't need was her weight on me, bearing me down. She slipped into the conversation, 'Listen, get

143

your stuff together and move into mine.'

That was the worst of it. I knew her game. Get me into the house, start charging me a bloody fortune. She had already told me she didn't want me turning up on her doorstep. But, as I had confided in her about my money, she was all ready for me to move in. I got out of her car and felt like absolute dog shit. In fact, worse than dog shit. Low. Really, really low. I thought, 'I do not want to speak to her again.'

I am on my own. I need to figure this out on my own. I had to forget about my stuff at her house. Just kiss that goodbye.

You know, she never called me to check on me.

I told Scott that I had gone to the doctors and that his attack on me had been reported to the police. I also told him that they had sent me to the abuse support group.

When Scott is faced with his own behaviour and he has to be held accountable for it, it does resonate with him. He was devastated that I had told anyone. He was ashamed, though it didn't stop him drinking and taking drugs. The physical abuse ended here, but not the psychological abuse.

I had found a councillor at the time that he attacked me. I was looking for help. It was a bit of a waste of time really. She didn't really have any advice for me concerning Scott's behaviour. But I did speak to her about my panic attacks. I had seen councillors before this and she was the first one to suggest that it could stem from childhood trauma.

This made complete sense to me. She suggested that some kind of trauma had happened to me as a child, and I had buried it away. This trauma had resurfaced as anxiety and panic attacks in my twenties. I never really understood why they were happening to me. From being strong, independent, travelling around on my own, not bothered about going anywhere alone, to being almost agoraphobic, using my phone as a crutch in case I had an attack. Certainly not able to drive distances in my car. I hated it.

For some reason, once I understood that about the panic attacks, I seemed to take control of them. I'm not saying that I don't have anxiety now, but I know when I am working and training too hard, I can feel that dread of doom. I know that I need to take my foot off the gas and nurture myself, be kind to myself. Slow down and evaluate why I feel the way I do. It doesn't take long for me to be back on my game and feeling better.

I had a few friends that I used to confide in. My mate Becky was one of them. She was my training buddy and was usually the first person that I would see after his horrendous behaviour. Becky knew what I was living in. She also knew that I had to leave him. Becky would never tell me what I needed to do. She would just listen and be there. She did one time show me a house that she owned with a buddy of hers. There was a room to rent. It was a lovely house and a great room to move into. But it only had one bathroom and toilet. I confided in her not so long ago about why I did not take that place at the time, because she quite often brings up the fact that you know you nearly took that place. Her showing me that place was showing me a way out of what I was in. Unfortunately, I wasn't ready. When you live with a narcissist, who is hell-bent on breaking you down, you do not realise the chip, chip, chip at your self-esteem. You do not realise that they make you feel like a worthless piece of shit, and like you are not worth anything to anyone.

This is going to sound utterly stupid, but I had a whole issue around taking a dump in other people's toilets. He made me believe that I was disgusting and that I stank and no one should have to live with that.

The only reason I did not take that room is because of the

house only having one toilet. So ridiculous now. We all shit. Shit stinks.

Men, all men take note. Women shit, all the time. Oh, and they fart. YES, that's right. We fart, and loud! You men do what you want, shit when you want, fart when you want. But, oh no, women, no women do not do such disgusting things. We are frilly and pretty and no, no, no, toilet stuff, that doesn't happen. So that was the end of that. I stayed. Becky never gave up though.

Dad was around on my Facebook, posting stupid shit. He posted at this time how thankful he was to have Leigh and Ashley in his life with all his grandchildren. Where was I in all this? I'll tell you where, no-fucking-where. Dad had come over from the US and visited his younger brother, who lives in Cornwall. Leigh got invited. Ashley was there too. My invite was obviously lost in the post.

Leigh phoned me up one day and told me Dad had cancer. It's sad to say this, but we both laughed. Leigh told me that Dad was going to call me. Dad did call me. He wittered on about how much he loved me and Leigh. I sat there listening to his bullshit down the phone. He wasn't telling me that to make me feel good. He was trying to exonerate himself from his own behaviour. Fucking arsehole. It was sickening. He then told me how he was leaving me his Harley Davidson in his will. I mean, what the fuck am I meant to do with that? Number one, I do not ride motorbikes; and two, how fucking much would it cost me to get it across from the USA? I didn't believe what he was saying anyway. What he says and what he does are two very different things. I put the phone down and that was the end of that. He got treated, he was fine. That was 2013. We didn't speak again until 2016.

My uncle Keith got in touch not long after that to tell me that

Gran had passed away (horrible Gran). He asked if I would come to the funeral. I made the time and went down to Cornwall and met up with Uncle Miles and Aunty Charlotte, who I hadn't seen since I was probably eleven. They didn't think I was going to go. They were really happy when I turned up. We all stood around taking the piss out of Dad. Uncle Miles, his eldest brother, said, 'Who the fuck does he think he is, with his cowboy boots and his American swag?'

I agreed and said, 'I know right, a fucking idiot!'

That's when Uncle Miles told me that they had tried to take me and Leigh. I told Leigh, and we both then wondered what life could have been like if we had people that actually loved us. I think we both feel there has been wasted time in trying to recover from the trauma of the abuse growing up.

I did send Dad a message. Just highlighting his inadequacies. How when people die, it should give you time to reflect. Reflect on things not said, things not done or achieved. I made a vow to myself back when I was twenty-eight: I will have no regrets. I will live and do everything I want to do. I will say what I want to say. A life not lived is not a life at all.

He didn't respond to me. I didn't want a response. He just needed to know how I felt and have his behaviour written down in black and white for him to read.

He didn't come to his mum's funeral.

Scott had a fight coming up; he was kind of focused. I mean, on reflection, he was up to all sorts. I was really now wiser to what he was doing. I just tried to get on with living, paying the bills and surviving. He told me that his opponent had pulled out and that he had been offered a fight that was another six kilos under what he needed to be. He had to lose it in four days. I told him it was stupid. He would do that ridiculous cutting the MMA

147

fighters do before a fight. It is so bad for you. It leaves you dehydrated and weak. I told him, 'What the fuck are you asking me for? You are going to do it anyway.'

He wanted my advice. I told him my advice. He didn't want to hear that. He wanted my advice on how to lose the weight in such a short amount of time. I said, 'Go find your other coach, the one that has said it's a good idea for you to take this fight,' because I wanted nothing to do with it.

So that was that. He lost the weight. I told him the morning of the fight I was not coming. He didn't think I was going to say no. I had started to find my strength a bit when it came to standing up to him. He went and fought and broke his ankle.

His mum, who was already struggling to look after his dad, was extremely upset that he had broken his ankle. He told her that he had done it whilst he was on a training day for the post office. I had to go along with it. He didn't want to tell her that he had done it in a fight.

Him breaking his ankle meant I was now ferrying him around making sure that he was taken care of, whilst I was still trying to make rent, pay bills and take care of both of us. This was also a time when he decided to get sick pay from the government. This pricked him up to thinking, 'Ooh, maybe I could just sign on anyway.'

'There is no fucking way. You are an able-bodied man that is able to work, you get a fucking job!'

He was always referring to the fact that he deserved it. He deserved to have money, deserved for good things to happen to him, deserved notoriety for acting. He just deserved it. Let me tell you something, nobody deserves anything without hard work and dedication to what they are doing. Unless you have been born into a family that has wealth that can give you whatever you want, the rest of us have to get off our asses and get out there and graft.

Scott's dad was now in hospital, and it looked like he was not going to make it out. Scott was spending more and more time supporting his mum, which was to be expected. It did also mean that he was not in the flat at all. It was lovely.

Scott's dad wasn't going to make it. The whole family was summoned down to the hospital. Scott's dad was basically taking his last breaths. We were all in the room with him when he left us.

Of course, it was sad, but it was also really peaceful. He was quiet and not suffering. There was a sense of relief. No more heart attacks and pills that were off the charts. He hadn't been able to leave the house for months and really had no quality of life. He was now resting.

We left the hospital and went to Scott's mum's house. What do you say? What do you do? There's an emptiness. Just try to pick up the pieces and get on with life. I stayed for a bit and then made my way back to the flat. Scott stayed with his mum to keep her company.

Two weeks had passed since Scott's dad's death. Scott phoned me and told me that he was now going to stay at his mum's. They had obviously talked about it without me. Not even considered how I was meant to be paying for the flat on my own. 'Right, OK! What about the flat? What am I meant to do with that?'

Scott suggested that I come and move in with them. It would be a great way to save some money.

I had to think about it for a moment. Realistically, I knew that I couldn't afford the flat on my own but just for a moment I thought, 'Could I stay at the flat on my own?'

We had so much debt – sorry, I had so much debt – to sort out there was no way I could do it on my own.

I agreed to move into his Mum's. In all truth, my self-worth was at an all-time low. I wasn't in a position to live with people I didn't know, and I still wasn't in a position to leave him. I'm not sure why. It would have been so easy then. I haven't got an answer.

I was cycling through Winton one day. I just parked my bike outside my usual health shop. I saw her walking towards me. I was going to get on my bike and make a run for it. It was Mum. I knew she had seen me. I waited until she had reached me. We exchanged pleasantries and she asked, 'You got time for a cuppa?'

'Sure.'

We walked across the road to a coffee shop, found a table and sat for a while, it was nice. She said, 'You obviously sorted it out with Scott?'

I lied, 'It was OK.'

I told her I was finishing my degree. I hadn't seen her in eighteen months. She would not have known that I started my BSc. We exchanged chit-chat, she mentioned my shoes and that I should come and get them. I said, 'Oh great. Yes, let me finish my degree.' (I was up to my neck in writing my dissertation) 'I'll come and get them then.'

That was that. She left, I left, everything was fine. She didn't call, she didn't check in, nothing.

I finished my degree. I could be a teacher now if I wanted to be. Fuck that careers advisor. I now had two degrees. I could do whatever the fuck I liked and I was not stupid!

Once I had tied up all the loose ends with the academic work, I made my way down to my mum's. I had a new car, it was a

150

black convertible smart car. It was awesome. I had my degree. I was off to collect my shoes.

Mum let me in. Her house has never changed. You instantly know when you are walking into a house where a person suffers with mental health. The outside is inside, meaning the house is just full of chaos. No carpet on the stairs; it had been that way for twenty years plus. Empty pots of paint, brushes, clothes, sandpaper, paint brushes, all strewn up the stairs. The hallway leading up to the kitchen had letters left unopened at the front door, clothes again strewn up the hallway on the floor, half a wall painted and never finished. As you walked into the kitchen, half the garden (dirt, garden pots, diggers, etc) was inside the kitchen. Dirt and general filth everywhere. There was a doorway that led into another room, supposedly a dining room, which was always stacked with shit: plants, papers, books, bike, piles of clothes, etc. That room led into the living room. The doorway was stacked with about twenty or thirty paint cans. Used, unused, who knows? You couldn't get through the door, that was for sure! The kitchen sides were always filthy. She asked if I wanted a cuppa. I said 'Sure.'

I tried to find what looked like the cleanest cloth to wipe the sides down. I washed the cups to within an inch of their lives, then sat and had a cuppa. I told her about my degree and how I could be a teacher now. She couldn't even look at me. At that point I was thirty-eight or thirty-nine. I was over getting validation from her. I just observed her behaviour. She had nothing for me. No, 'Well done!' No, 'Amazing Janine, I am really proud of you!' Nothing. I didn't need it. Everything I have done has been for me. I validate myself. Fuck her, and fuck her bullshit.

I could only really manage a short amount of time with her.

It was just so draining! 'Right, it's time to go.'

I asked for my shoes as she was showing me some shelves she had put together. She looked surprised. She held her hand to her chest and said, 'OH, I gave them all to the cats protection charity.'

I fucking looked at her. I didn't get angry. I didn't say anything. My internal conversation in my head was this:

'I AM DONE. I WILL NEVER SEE YOU AGAIN. I AM NEVER COMING BACK TO THIS HOUSE AS LONG AS I LIVE.'

She then went on to say, 'You should have seen the lady in the shop, she loved the shoes.'

I said, 'Well, they were all brand-new. I'm sure she did. OK, Mum, I'm off, see you later.'

That was the last time I saw her. She has never tried to call me. She could find me if she needed to. I am well known in my small town. It would not have been difficult to find me.

It wasn't about the shoes; it was about the sheer vindictiveness of her actions. How much punishment does one person have to take for something they have never done?

I was now at the flat, trying to tidy it up, leave it in some kind of semblance of order. I didn't have the money to clean the carpets, but I could paint. So that's what I did. That fucker did not help me with any of it. I didn't expect him too. I painted every single room in the flat, bar the living area because some roof work needed doing. In-between work and training I was painting the flat. The flat belonged to our friends. I didn't want them to think we were complete assholes.

Scott did not give a flying monkey's what they thought, and he certainly didn't give a fuck about helping me clear it up.

I was now living at his mum's. I had my own room. He had

his room. We didn't sleep in the same bed. My room there was a little bit of sanctuary away from his nonsense. He had not long finished his first film.

He was now a filmmaker. He decided that he wasn't getting the parts at the auditions that he was going to. He wrote a screenplay. Scavenged around for people to give him money to make the film. Used me to buy the food and feed the film crew. Of course I was doing this, in amongst trying to pay bills, rent, etc. I'm an idiot. I just said, 'Yes. I'll do it.'

He directed it, starred in it and wrote it.

I mean, I am always proud of what someone does when they work hard for it. Scott did work hard at putting the film together.

If I remember correctly, the first film was a play first. The play was very good. But this is what Scott does. He takes from everyone he has around him. He burns his bridges and then nobody wants to help him with anything. He had burnt his bridges with most of his friends because he saw them as commodities. Used them, took what he needed and then threw them away.

A friend of mine at the time asked me if I wanted to start a weightlifting club. I said 'Sure.'

We set up a club at the gym I was working at as a PT. Three nights a week. It was really cool. It was quite successful. I always had students coming through the door. This is when I got my invitation to compete at the British Championships in Olympic lifting. You get invited to the British Champs, you don't enter. I was forty and knew that this would be the last time I would be able to make it to the senior championship before I would be relegated to the masters. I was getting old and I knew the weights that I was lifting would just not be enough to keep competing at senior level.

153

I was going to be competing with some of the Olympic athletes. I was so chuffed. I do not have any regrets in my life, because I have done and achieved some amazing things. But, if only I had been pushed into a sport in my youth.... who knows? I may have made it as an Olympic athlete. Just maybe.

Doesn't matter though. This comp would be the next best thing for me. It was in Bangor and I was game. I'm not going to go through the finer details of a lifting comp, it's pretty dull. I lifted. I didn't win. It doesn't matter. I was still on the podium with a bronze medal. There were only three in my category. I didn't care. I was stood up there, aged forty with teenage girls feeling proud as punch. I had my medal and soaked it all up. Another tick box achieved.

That was the end of me competing in the seniors. I was now officially a masters lifter, competing with my peers at my own age.

Life at Scott's mum's just ticked along. Although, one day he announced that he wasn't going to work any more, he was going to sign on the dole. I said, 'No way!'

I was so incensed. He was an able-bodied man who could work and not become a drain to our system that is set up for people that that are desperate. HE DID NOT WANT TO WORK BECAUSE IT DIDN'T SUIT HIS FILM MAKING LIFESTYLE! This led to a massive fight in his mother's home. We were in my room, where the discussion was getting more and more heated until I lunged at him. I was the aggressor this time. That this fucking human just didn't want to think about anyone else other than himself enraged me. I one hundred percent at that moment hated him, he was so fucking selfish. If I'm honest I hated him all the time at that point. Scott's mum could hear us from down stairs. She of course was horrified, and rightly so.

Living at his mum's I realised that his mum was his enabler to his behaviour. She never said 'No' to him. Whatever he asked for, she gave him.

One evening when he was out who knows where, she was heading off to bed. She was about to go back up the stairs, when she popped her head back in the door, 'Umm, Janine, Scott hasn't got any sheets on his bed.'

'Right.'

'Well, they will get all stinky.'

'Scott is a big boy and Scott can change his own sheets.'

She wasn't happy about it.

'If Scott can't be bothered to change his own sheets, that is Scott's problem.'

Off she went. Of course, what she wanted me to do was go up there and change his sheets and sort his room out. Fuck that. I was done picking up his shit and chasing around after him. I had taken to picking up his dirty underpants off the floor and just putting them straight back in the drawer. He didn't fucking care. I mean, it was just too much work to put them in the wash basket. So fuck him.

I'd been living there a good eight months and came home from work one day to Scott's mum making lunch. She had two plates out. One for her and one for him. She looked at me surprised, 'Oh, I wasn't expecting you,' were her words.

'Funny that, because I live here!'

I knew then, right from that moment what her agenda was. Just tiny little acts like that can tell you everything about a person.

Scott came through the door and she said, 'I've made you lunch.'

He turned his nose up at it. 'I don't want it, give it to Janine.'

I laughed and sat there and ate it all up, in my belly!

Scott's drinking had really started to pick up pace again. I was finding litre bottles of vodka everywhere. His favourite thing to do was to come into my room first thing on a Sunday morning, around six thirty a.m., my only day off, and bring me breakfast. Yes, yes, I should not be so ungrateful. Yes, it is very nice to get breakfast in bed. But, he did not do it for me. He was doing it because he was bored of being on his own drinking all night and wanted to sit at the end of my bed and rant all his opinions at me in his pissed-up state. The shit that I had to listen to was exhausting. The rest of the day would be spent with him recovering or continuing drinking. We never went anywhere and never did anything. Our whole life circulated around his addiction. It was incredibly lonely and isolating.

I had started speaking to a couple of my close friends about him. He didn't like that too much. He would say, 'Stop telling them about me!'

'Well stop being a fucking wanker then!'

I don't really know what happened to me whilst I was living at his mum's. I had started to find my strength. I didn't care what he was doing. I was at my happiest when he was out taking drugs, fucking women and doing whatever else it was that he was doing, because it meant that he was not at home bothering me.

Everyone looked at good old Scott as the happy-go-lucky funny man. This is the identity that he presented. That's why he didn't like me telling people how he really was because it would blow his cover.

Scott announced one day, 'I'm coming off Facebook.'

'Right, what have you done?'

'Nothing! I'm just coming off of it. I've had enough, I need a break.'

'Right,' I said, 'I know you have done something and I do

not care, I do not give a fuck!'

Scott had decided that we should renew our vows. It was coming up to our ten-year anniversary. I, as usual, would go along with everything. I think I might have mentioned that if he was going to do it he needed to sort it out yourself. I wasn't spending the day cooking and catering for everyone.

Scott hired out a local nightclub, and invited quite a few of our friends. He had even sorted out a vicar coming down to do our vows. It was quite the show.

Let's move forward a few weeks from the Facebook announcement. It is the day of the renewing of the vows. I am driving him down to the party. He tells me in the car he has a confession.

I knew it, I knew that he had done something. He then proceeded to tell me that a woman may turn up at the party because he had been telling her how much he loved her. Probably fucking her. Who knows? I just didn't care. He wasn't fucking me and there was no way that I was giving that up any time soon.

'You are a fucking twat! If she turns up, I will invite her in and introduce her to everyone, telling everyone at that party who the fuck she is!'

He looked surprised at my response. 'You wouldn't dare.'

'You have lived with me for ten years and you don't know that I wouldn't do that? You know that I would do that!'

We arrived at the party. I have to put my showtime face on and pretend like nothing is happening. Just like nothing had been happening for ten years.

Nobody knew a thing.

About three weeks before the renewal of the vows, I had been training with a friend of mine, early in the morning. I was tired, but as usual I was pushing myself and not listening to my body. I was weightlifting and in the warm up I was jumping on a metal jump box. On one of the jumps my foot clipped the edge of the box. I missed the jump and smashed my shin on the edge of the box. It hurt, but I just carried on training.

It then started to throb. I decided to lift up my leggings to take a look. It wasn't pretty. I had a massive chunk of skin missing from my shin, and most of the skin was missing from the whole of my leg all the way up to my knee. I asked my friend if there was a first aid box. He pointed down to the office where he followed me. When I pulled up my trouser leg, he took one look at it and went green. I laughed. I wrapped that bad boy up and finished my session.

The wound bled for three days. I then realised that it was infected. I had a whole issue with the doctors. The nurse thought that the scab on the top was OK and that it was healing. It wasn't; it was festering under the scab.

After the party at the club, a group of our friends had gone back to one of their houses. Drugs were being passed around. Loads of smoking was taking place. I fucking hate smoking. As I was sat in amongst the chaos going on around me I could smell my leg. I knew then that something wasn't quite right. I had had enough off the façade and wanted out. I wanted to be on my own. I made my exit and fucked off home.

I'm not sure if he stayed out all night. Probably. I was off down the hospital the following day because a stinky wound on your body is not a good wound that is healing. I needed someone to look at it. I ended up having to go the district nurse every day for dressing.

Not long after this, while I was riding to work, I felt a strange pain in my right knee. Since the ACL rupture and meniscus tear, my knee has never been the same. I am always very aware of it, very nervous around it. I do not let it stop me from doing what I want to do, and let me tell you, I have tested it since I ruptured it. I certainly haven't used it as an excuse or weakness to say no to doing anything. It just isn't as strong as it should be and is definitely weaker because of the injury.

I ignored the pain and kept on riding. But something definitely wasn't right. I think I may well have torn it slightly at training with the weights, when I was pulling the bar off the floor. Anyway, I went to the gym one day. There was a little something on the side of my knee, under the skin, that was bothering me. There were always bits floating around. I just used to push them around until it didn't feel uncomfortable any more. I sat down on the seated row, pushed something on my knee and that was it. I don't know what happened, but my knee locked up. I tried to walk over to the matts to stretch it out. But I could barely walk. I then tried to get on the bike to see if I could flush it out. That didn't work either. I was now in so much pain. I hobbled down to the physio unit where I worked to see if one of the physios could straighten it out.

She did sort of straighten my leg out. I was still in so much pain. I hobbled home, hoping that a good night's sleep might make it relax, and I would wake up and everything would be good again.

My knee was fucked, again. It was now the next day. I was limping around the kitchen, with a full day of personal training and weightlifting coaching ahead of me. I knew full well how fucking hard it was going to be, I was now a leg down, again. I crumpled up on the sideboard in the kitchen with my head buried in my arm and sobbed. I knew my knee was fucked.

I brushed myself down, made myself breakfast and got on with my day the best I could. No point sitting around moaning

159

about it. It is what it is. I've got the rest of my body to use.

I got one of the physios I knew to write me a referral to see my consultant, who had fixed it originally. There was no question about whether I had torn something. He got me into the surgery straight away. My third operation on that knee. I thought, 'Get the op done, get back to rehab. Get it strong again.'

I know that I am not the best person to look after. I do need to be told to slow down. I also need someone that can just do stuff for me without asking for it. You know, just support you when you are down. Our relationship was never built on him supporting me. It was always me supporting him. If I asked for any help, he would always fuck it up by being wasted or losing the keys to the car or completely forgetting that he had to do anything. To be honest, I never really asked for help.

On this one occasion I did ask for help. I couldn't drive. I was only two days out of surgery and I had to go and coach an Olympic lifting session. There were people that relied on me, and I did not want to let them down. I asked for him to pick me up so that I could get home. His response was that he was out filming late. I knew that it was a crock of shit. I mean, why should I expect anything less. I mean, never mind that I had paid and fed all of his film crew, ran around for him making sure that everything was taken care of, and prepared the rooms for his actors to stay in. His room was always a shit pit. He was taking so many steroids at this point as well. I cleared out the draw next to his bed because it was full of used needles and empty vials. Once I emptied it out, I had a bin liner full of used steroid shit. I sat there looking at the bag thinking, 'That selfish cunt. All that money. I am trying to pay off debt and bills accrued by him as well.'

He just didn't give a fuck.

I got a friend at the weightlifting club to give me a lift in the end. They dropped me at the end of the road, I limped back to the house and went straight to bed. I didn't really see Scott until Sunday morning, with the usual poached eggs on toast at six thirty a.m. He'd probably been on the vodka since Friday night. He took his usual position at the bottom of my bed, and started his pissed-up ranting. I would lay there looking at him with utter contempt.

He then proceeded to confess that he hadn't been out filming late. He was on a date with a twenty-four-year-old girl. I told him he was a fucking pig. He then told me that it made him realise that he did not want to be with her and that he wanted to be with me. Like he was doing me a favour. I mean, the bloke was a fucking idiot. I fucking hated him. He just couldn't see that his behaviour was the undoing in our relationship.

I was the bad guy. I was the one not putting out. I mean, you know, what was he meant to do? He had to get it from somewhere.

I am sure around this time, I had said to him, 'We are done. I do not want this any more. I do not want to be with you any more!'

He had kind of agreed, but really, he never thought that I would leave.

Self-reflection is really important. Looking at yourself and analysing your own behaviour. How have you grown? If you keep repeating the same mistakes, you need to ask yourself: why? How was I in this relationship with this person? I had started to realise that I was being manipulated. There was no way that he was going to kill himself. I soon realised that there were parallels with my relationship with my mum and the relationship with Scott.

When you grow up in dysfunction, it becomes the norm. You replicate the behaviour and the relationships that you have with people. Boyfriends and girlfriends.

There was the epiphany: the abuse was exactly the same. I needed out. I looked out of my bedroom window and thought, 'This can't be the rest of my life. I want to go!'

It was then that I saw the way out. I had the strength and the clarity to see the light out of the hell hole I was living in.

Seeing the Light

I can count my close friends on a single hand.

Becky, who had tried previously to guide me out of the relationship, was the person I turned to first. I asked her if she knew of any flats that I could start to look at. She was all over it, right out of the bat. I looked at the first property. It was OK, but I didn't like it. Becky then told me of a place that she had in Stafford Road, right in the centre of town. It wouldn't be ready for two weeks because she was doing a refurb on it. But I could take a look at it and see what I thought.

I went to Stafford Road that same day. I knew straight away that I wanted to live there. Three double rooms, all en suite. Centre of town with a big back garden, ten minutes away from the beach. Becky told the builders that the front bedroom had to be finished first so that I could move. The rest they could finish while I set myself up in the front room.

Scott somehow found out. I'm not sure how. I didn't care. I was done!

He begged and pleaded. Sat by my bed every night, 'Let's talk, I want to talk.'

'There is nothing to talk about. How many times have I told you, I am leaving! Well, this time I am. I am done. I have given you eleven years of my life!'

Over the years I knew I had become a broken record. 'If you do that again, I am leaving.' I never left. I honestly think he thought I would never leave. That he had done enough work on me to make me believe no one else would want me.

At the point of me seeing my way out of the shit, I honestly did not give a shit if no one else wanted me. I would rather be on my own, than be in this hell hole of a life with a narcissistic bipolar alcoholic, injected up to the eye balls on steroids.

The two weeks at his mum's house were hell. I stayed strong. I had found myself. I knew there was a new life waiting ahead of me. On the day of my moving he drove up in his car and again pleaded with me not to go. I told him 'NO. I am out of here!'

He pulled away in his car wailing. I could still hear him at the junction down the road. I am sorry to say that I laughed. I had no empathy or compassion left for that human being. He had drained every ounce of that out of me over the eleven years we had been together.

I packed up my car, took what I could fit in my tiny little Peugeot and got the fuck out of there!

I left with my clothes, shoes, laptop and eleven years of debt.

I WAS FREE!

There isn't any amount of money you can put on that. I had my freedom.

Being In My Base

I set up in my room, that was my base. Everything I owned was in that room. I had no kitchen wares, no furniture other than a mattress that I managed to buy with a credit card. Becky dropped off a base for the bed. Beggars can't be choosers, so I was super appreciative of it. But when you sat on it, the noise it made from the springs certainly meant I was not going to be seeing any action on that without waking up the whole neighbourhood!

I was set though. All I needed was a place to get my head down, a shower, and a place to cook my food. All the rest would come in good time.

I was in that flat on my own for a good four months before I started to rent out the other rooms. The first few weeks of being in there was nerve-wracking. Every single sound I heard, I thought was Scott. I spent a lot of my nights running up and down my hallway with a set of nunchucks I had left over from my training days at The Bulldog. I tried to do a stint at learning how to use them. I also had a baton in the other hand. I was ready. If he was coming to get me, I was ready fight.

I had no curtains in the living area and kitchen. I convinced myself he was hiding in the bushes at the back of my house. There is nothing more unnerving at night time than when you think they can see in but you can't see out. I had to get that sorted quick smart; get those curtains up so that no one could see in.

A couple of weeks after I had left Scott, me and Becky saw him parked up round the corner of where I was living. He did not

165

look well. Like, mentally not well. He had his top off, sweaty, looking like he had not slept for the two weeks I had been gone. It was the beginning of December, so it was bloody freezing! He had a look of the insanity about him. That didn't do me any favours for being in the flat on my own. I stayed strong though and took every day as it came. I started to get on with my new life.

He turned up at my work place a couple of times. Still begging me to come back to him. 'Let's talk!'

I had to reiterate: I was done with talking, there was nothing left!. He made all his usual promises. 'I'll be better, I'll do better.' I did not believe a word of it!

This is when I started receiving pages and pages of hand written letters left on my car, or he would find a way to put them inside in my car. These letters would go through trying to get me on-side and then just plain nasty horrible personal shit.

He then told me that he was going to get the divorce sorted and that he would pay for it. I thought that that was the least he could do, after the amount of money he had rinsed out of me over eleven years. He asked for my address, as he needed it for the forms. I stupidly believed him. I sent him my details. Nothing came of it. He was trying everything he could to open up communication with me.

I knew right from the get-go that all communication had to be severed. He would try to manipulate me. Talk me round, do everything he could do to get me to come back. There was no way that I was going to let that happen. By giving him my address details on the assumption he was actually going to do something good, he knew exactly where I was living.

2014/2015 was my first Christmas on my own in eleven years. I was so excited. I was studying hard with my masters. I had Christmas Day on my own set up. I was going to study in the morning, go and have dinner with my brother and then make my way over to Becky's house for an evening catch up with her family.

The day couldn't have been any more perfect for me. Just pottering around, pleasing myself. When I woke in the morning, I looked into changing my name back to my maiden name. I thought you had to be divorced in order to change your name. It turns out it cost fifteen pounds and I could do it by deed poll. It was the best fifteen pounds I had spent and the best Christmas present to myself. I was now Janine Davis again. I was back to being me!

Christmas cruised along. I floated around until New Year's Eve. My friend Debs invited me over to her house for a party. I was in two minds, but at the last minute decided to go. Everyone was drinking heavily; I was still on the no-drinking vibe. I wasn't ready yet to let my hair down. Debs and her friends kept shoving drinks at me. I would be gracious in taking them and then discreetly place them down without them seeing. I was being quizzed by her sister about my life in general. When people find out that you used to be a fighter, they have all kinds of questions they want to ask you. She also started to quiz me on if I was with anyone.

I told her I had just left my alcoholic husband. It was funny because I wasn't ashamed any more. I was in a place where I could share the truth about all of it. I told them that we hadn't had sex for over ten years. It felt so liberating to just be open about all of it. To tell my story. I was in a place where I just didn't care if people wanted to judge me. I had set myself free, not only of the abusive relationship, but of all the shame and hiding the truth that came with that toxic relationship.

167

Debs was pushing this guy Leon on me. She kept introducing us. He wasn't my type at all. They were all getting more and more drunk. I spent my time avoiding Leon. As the night wore on, we decided to all head down to the beach to see the fireworks. Leon was trying to give me his coat because he thought I looked cold. I told him I was fine, thank you. I didn't need his coat.

The next thing I knew, I was being pulled over by Leon, Debs' sister and Marve. They were colluding to go into to town but only wanted this select group to go; it felt pretty cool that they had asked me. We ditched everyone, got in my car and headed into town. We spent the night bar hopping and just having the utmost fun. I did for a brief moment think, 'If Scott sees me out with these guys, he will go ape shit,' but fuck it, I was having fun.

Leon was really turning it up now. It was getting on for five or six in the morning. He was getting really close and touchy feely. I embraced it. It was nice to have someone in to me. I hadn't experienced that in over eleven years. Debs' sister, Marve and Leon all ended up back at my place. It was so empty. I had nothing in the fridge, nothing in the cupboards, rooms empty. Even Marve was surprised. He said, 'My place is sparse as a bachelor but your place is a whole level up.'

When I say I left Scott with nothing, I really mean nothing. Unless you have had the experience of leaving an abusive relationship, you will not truly understand what it means to have to start your whole life all over again.

Leon made his play for me. He kissed me as I was showing him around my place. It was nice, awkward, but nice. He asked me if he should stay or go. I thought about it for five minutes and said, 'sure, stay.'

It was nice to have some intimacy. We didn't have sex. We

just kissed and cuddled. Talked and slept. Looking back at myself around that time, I was so vulnerable.

Leon took my number and said we should have a weekend in Brighton. I was like 'Sure.'

Leon introduced me to WhatsApp. I didn't know anything about WhatsApp. The funny thing as well is he had asked for me to put some tunes on. I showed him my CD collection. No one was listening to CDs any more. I must have looked like a right dork!

He also tried to put his arm around me when we were walking down the road the following day to go into town for a cuppa. He asked me if it made me uncomfortable. Why do people have this preconceived idea that I do not like to be close or cuddle? It must be my aura that I give off. If I like the person touching me, I do not have an issue! I did say to him, 'Why would I have a problem?' But I did mention that he might want to think twice about doing it, because if my ex-husband was hiding close to where I lived, he was likely to smash the shit out of him'.

Leon tried to big himself up, 'Yeah, I can handle that!'

I told him, 'You are, what, seventy-eight to eighty-five kilos? Ex-husband is one hundred and eighteen kilos and really fucking strong.' Leon soon let go of me and we went and hid in a café in town where no one could see us.

It wasn't long before Leon started to send me pictures of his dick. I found it all very hilarious. You men are so weird. I'm not sure what you think we do with these pictures or even why you send them. I reciprocated with some ass shots. I don't care about taking my clothes off. It is just the naked body. I mean, who really cares!

One of my friends who had been out in the single market for a while had tried to warn me. 'Don't send any pictures.'

'Too late for that one.'

Like I said, I do not care. I do not have skeletons in my cupboard. I have done a lot of crazy shit, and I am not ashamed to talk about it or hide it. I was a grown woman, who was in pretty good shape for her age. If I wanted to send this dude pictures of my bare ass, I was going to.

Just before the weekend to Brighton. Leon sent me a one minute and three second clip of his erect penis ejaculating. It was very strange.

I did say to him, 'What do you want me to do with that?' There was so much cum; it went on forever. Is it ego? Or was he so proud of his penis that day that he wanted to share it with me? Who the fuck knows? I know what you are thinking, I should have binned him. That is a definite sign of something not being right. But you know like I have said before, I was fresh out of the dysfunction. I was still not in a place where I should have questioned that behaviour.

Anyway, I booked my train. I was off to Brighton to get my rocks off. Something I hadn't done in eleven years.

I arrived in Brighton and Leon met me at the train station. I realise now he had a whole role of behaviour set out right from the start. I knew it at the time. I also knew I was there for one thing and one thing only: SEX. I suppose in my deluded fantasy, I believed he wanted to be with me and that it might develop into something else. It turns out at that time, I was still an idiot.

Leon took my bag, because clearly I was struggling to carry it myself. What is with that? Why do I have to give into that behaviour of men. Yes, I know they are being very gentlemanly, but really, do I look weak and feeble? Can I not carry my own bag? Have we not moved on from the women being the weaker sex? I mean, I am a former world champion Thai boxer and I have picked up 185 kilos off the floor. I think I can manage a bag that weighs five kilos.

I give in though. I want him to feel like the man he wants to be. The man that sent me a one minute and three second clip of him ejaculating. He clearly needed validation of his manhood. Leon took me for something to eat, and started to berate me about eating healthy. I ignored it and just chose what I liked to eat, because I do not like to eat shit. (KFC, McDonalds or anything associated with that fuck-hole of shit food that is the reason that most of the western world is in an obesity epidemic!)

He suggested that we dump our stuff at the hotel and then take a look around Brighton. I let him pay for the hotel, fuck him. He had chosen well; the hotel was pretty funky and the room was really cool. Round bed, retro white and orange furniture with an alcove you could sit in where you could look out over the square and people watch.

Leon liked to smoke weed. I'm not good on weed. I had long since given up smoking that twenty-plus years ago. He insisted in the room that I have some. I tried to say no, but he persisted.

I said, 'Right, I will only take in the passive smoke, and if I get weird you have to look after me!' That was the deal. There was no smoking in the room, so we hid in the shower so that the smoke would be extracted out by the fan. It felt good being naughty again. I was allowed just to be me. The weed didn't hit me that hard. I just felt happy.

We went for a little walk around the town, and he suggested that we get a drink.

I said, 'You know what, I want an alcoholic drink!' It would be my first vodka in fifteen years. Now was the time to just let go and be free.

I ordered a vodka and cranberry juice with ice and a squeeze

171

of lime. It tasted so good. Leon was starting to get very sexually flirty with me. We made our way back to hotel. I also bought some more vodka for the room. I was on a roll. A buddy of mine checked in with me. Wanted to make sure that I was OK. I told her I was smoking weed and drinking vodka, life was good. My buddy voiced her concerns. These people that question my fragility make me laugh. I may well have not been drinking for the past fifteen years but I had endured a relationship with an alcoholic, along with becoming a world champion twice over. I am sure a few drinks were not going to kill me.

I know my constitution, and I know as long as I stick to the one drink, I will be absolutely fine. Vodka I can drink until the cows come home, which is a touch ironic, since the choice of demon for the ex-husband was vodka.

Now, I am not going to go into detail of what happened in the hotel room that afternoon. I am sure you can well imagine what we were up to. But, I will share this. Before we got down to sexual business, He challenged me to a push-up contest. I mean, what the fuck! I engaged. I also let him win. Made him feel like the man he should be. He also dragged me off the bed. I was in prone position, which is face down, with only my feet on the bed. He was holding my arms. My lower spine felt like it was going to snap in two. I told him, 'Fucking hell, that's painful!'

'I thought you were strong?'

'Fuck you, get on the bed I'll do the same to you!' He yelped like a little piggy. Idiot!

Whilst we were cavorting, I could see that he was trying to position himself. I did wonder what he was doing. He managed to wedge his feet into a certain position and then proceeded to smash my noo-noo to bits. In my head I was like, ok, this is new. No one has ever tried that before.

I thought 'Well, I am conditioned. I'll let him bang away.' I then unexpectedly laughed out loud in his face. I'm not sure why I did that, but what the fuck was he doing? I got my focus back again and let him finish.

When we were sat on the bed chatting, he proceeded to tell me about all the dates he had on the dating websites. I soon realised he was a prolific internet dater. He tells the women what they want to hear, fucks them, and then moves on to the next one. I'm not sure why he felt he could share this with me, but he did. Then confess the particular move that he was smashing the shit out of me with was one he likes to do with women because it makes them piss themselves. Leon then included that he wasn't sure why he was telling me all this. I do have a way of making people feel that they can tell me anything. Thankfully, I was not part of the gang of women he was making piss themselves.

The weekend went along swimmingly. Leon was trying his hardest to get me stoned to no avail. We went out to dinner, he questioned me about laughing in his face. I replied, 'I was enjoying myself so much.' It was a lie of course. Really, I should have just asked him what the fuck he thought he was doing.

Back at the hotel room, he was picking me apart, questioning my physique while I was naked. His behaviour was not too dissimilar to Scott's, but at a lower level. It didn't faze me one bit. I just saw a very insecure man. You know, we were sex funky. I hadn't put any deodorant on, my pheromones were flying. I didn't care. He obviously found it distasteful, as he suggested that he buy me some perfume. Dick! He also waved his penis around in my face. I hate it when guys do that. Wave their member around in your face, expecting to shove that thing in your mouth. I told him if that was going to happen he needed to take care of business down there for me. His response was, 'I DON'T DO THAT ONCE IT'S BEEN FUCKED!'

After he had waved that mother-fucking thing around my

chops, I got up and basically sat on his face with my noo. Fuck you!

Honestly though, I was still having a good time.

Leon also asked me if he had made me cum. Now, a forty year old man should know if that has happened. I didn't think anything of it. I thought about it for a minute and said, 'No but I have had a lovely time.' You know that his ego was in tatters. Why did you need to ask, idiot!

The following day we headed out for breakfast. This time I was stoned. I sat outside this coffee shop watching this woman walking towards me. I thought, 'She looks like one of Scott's film crew.' She did all the make- up for both of his films. I thought, 'No. I'm seeing things.' As she got closer, it was her. Can you believe it? I cannot go anywhere without knowing someone. She was cool, though. We had a little chat, and she wished me well. Leon shit himself. I then went and found my way to the train station to get home.

I never saw Leon again. He did call me a couple of weeks later. He wanted to tell me that he was coming to Bournemouth with another woman. Just in case we bumped into each other. Such a dick.

I said, 'Well, Bournemouth is a pretty big place, so I doubt that will happen.' He then asked what I had been doing. I thought, 'Fuck you, I know what you are doing.' I told him. I had seen this guy and that guy. He then got all narky and told me that maybe I could find someone to make me cum. I replied, 'Well you fucking never did!'

He got right on his high horse and said, 'I make women weak at the knees and make them piss themselves!'

'Well thank goodness I am not part of your piss gang!'

Fuck you, fuck off, that was the end of that!

It's Time to Get Shit-Faced

I was working hard with my master's. It was slowly starting to makes sense to me. Academia does not come easy. I am not an intellectual, not by any means. I did feel like a fraud most of the time I was at Bournemouth University. I never felt like I belonged there. Higher education only happened to people that came from affluent backgrounds. If you were from a council estate, you were and are the lowest of the low. You are never meant to amount to anything.

I often got asked where I was taking my master's. I would reply Bournemouth. These people would then inform me where they had done theirs like it was a competition as to where you got your master's. As if to say Bournemouth wasn't that great and they had a better master's than me. Fucking idiots. I would say nothing, in the hopes that they would go away and stop talking to me.

Working at a private tennis club, you come up against these types of people all the time. The upper middle class. The self-entitled assholes that look down their noses at anyone that doesn't drive around in a range rover and doesn't have a house in Sandbanks. For business, it is a great place to work, but most of them are so up their own assholes they can't see the woods for the trees.

All trying to fit in with the cliques. All wearing the one-hundred-pound leggings that you are going to sweat in when you go to the gym. I couldn't give a monkey's chuff.

175

All I know is that I have the aptitude to figure stuff out, or try to figure stuff out. I'm not a genius and I'm not that clever. But, I will give it a good go and see where it takes me.

I received an email one day from the university saying they were going to close down the account and not let me finish the master's. I was gobsmacked. What the fuck! WHY? I needed to speak to my supervisor. They had said in the email that I hadn't submitted this particular form that assesses how you are getting on with your research. I knew that I had because I had sat with my supervisor discussing the form and he had said that he would take care of it. Three years of work and all my money that I had paid literally going down the pan. I phoned the uni, but I was not getting any joy. The admin office people were not that helpful and basically said there was nothing they could do.

I went up to the uni and was sat in one of the courtyards in bits. I saw Dave, who I used to work with at The Litten Tree. He was pretty good mates with Scott at this point, and he asked if I was all right. I explained what was happening and that I couldn't talk. In fact I was fucking devastated. Dave left, and said, 'I hope you get it sorted out!'

I'm calling and calling I finally managed to speak to my supervisor. He had forgotten to send the form to the relevant people. The one address details I hadn't changed was the university. It just hadn't even crossed my mind. The university had sent a letter out five months previous to my old address. Scott's mum's address. Scott hadn't had the decency to forward it on to me. Fortunately, I got it all sorted out and continued with my research and getting that master's finished.

That night after I came out of coaching at Phoenix MMA, (I should tell you that Machine Martial Arts moved to The Phoenix MMA gym in Bournemouth, where I have now been teaching for twelve years) I found a card that had been slid through my car window. It was from Scott. He was sorry to hear what had happened with the uni. He had put a tea bag and an anti-psychotic pill in the card. The pill was supposed to be humourous, as a peace offering. He wrote that if there was anything he could do I should give him a shout.

That piece of shit Scott. I found out later that Dave had called him the day he had seen me. He told Scott I was in bits and that the uni was going to take me off my course. Dave knew that Scott had received that letter months before that situation. He asked him if he had sent it on to me. Of course he hadn't. But that motherfucker wanted to now help me. He knew exactly what he was doing. It's a boy thing, of course. Dave was loyal to his mate, he didn't want to drop him in it, but also knew that he hadn't given that letter to me.

Well, fuck you. It didn't work. I finished my master's.

Once that was all sorted, I could concentrate on the European championship. I had competed at the British Weightlifting Championships, that qualified me to enter the Europeans. They were being held in Bangor, Wales. Right on my doorstep. No flying across to Europe somewhere. I had competed at the university in Bangor before, so I knew where to stay and how to keep it cheap.

Lifting really isn't that exciting to talk about. You either lift it or you don't, and hope that your grouping doesn't have anyone in it that is lifting weights that are completely out of your league. I saw the opening numbers go up for my group and thought, 'I am in for a chance of a win here. I just need to be sensible with my opening numbers and make sure I do not mess my lifts up.'

I didn't go for any PB's. I played it safe enough to get the win. If you go on YouTube, you will find me getting interviewed; it's hilarious. The guy standing with me is not my coach. I didn't have a coach. I was my own coach. He was just my mate that came to support me.

European Masters Weightlifting Champion, another boxed ticked.

It was now time for me to get shit-faced. I needed to go out and just let rip. I asked my mate if she wanted to come out with me. She was totally up for it. I wanted to get out of town as well. I didn't want to bump into any clients, or Scott, or anyone who knew Scott. I wanted to be somewhere where nobody knew me. I did not want to be judge or questioned or hear, 'Oh my god, have you seen Janine?' I had built a reputation now for clean living. No drinking, eating shit or anything else that comes along with not looking after yourself.

I get judged if I am eating a bar of chocolate. 'Ooh, is that chocolate you are eating? aren't you bad?'

'Oh, fuck off and worry about your own life style and stop judging mine,' I think. Of course, I keep that to myself.

I nod quietly. 'Yes, yes, bad me I'm eating chocolate.' So the last thing I needed was anyone seeing me completely out of it.

Both me and my friend decided we were all in. Drink and drugs. I just wanted to escape reality for just a moment. I know, don't judge me. Just a little bit of MDMA.. You know they use MDMA for PTSD. It just lets you float about for a bit. All your inhibitions dissolve away and you just feel really cosy and just want to dance your little socks off.

As it had been quite a few years since I had done anything like that, we were going to run a trial night. Just have a few drinks. Take a little bit, see how we got on. If it went tits-up we were not too far away from home.

It was the first time in ages I was able to let go of the control. I had been focused for over fifteen years on winning titles and studying hard. I just wanted to be free.

Four shots of Jägermeister, a bomb of MDMA (just a small

178

amount) and we were off. First club was Halo. I was really starting to fly. I felt on top of the world. This was my first introduction to the Jäger bomb. 'What's a Jäger bomb?'

My mate replied, 'Don't worry. Get this down you.'

I hadn't realised that there was a cup inside the cup. I ended up with most of the Jäger bomb all down my front. Off to the toilets. I had to go down some very slippery stairs where I managed to miss the last five steps on to the dance floor, I somehow manged to hold on to the banister with my hands and comfortably land on my feet. I let go and casually strutted off to the toilets.

Out of Halo, now on to The Winchester, feeling like a queen. I spent most of my time strutting around the dance floor in a floaty world of my own. My mate was talking to this young man and called me over. She told me what his name was.

'Septimus.'

It stopped me in my tracks. I stood still for a minute. I screwed up my face and said, 'What?'

He replied, 'Septimus.'

We both looked at each other and laughed. MDMA makes you very honest. You will say what you see. Which can been seen as very rude, but honestly, how many Septimuses do you come across? EVER!

Me and Septimus got to chatting and out of the blue he said, 'Do you want to fuck me?'

I replied, 'Do you want to fuck me?'

He looked at me like, 'Of course I fucking do!'

I thought about it for a minute and thought, what the fuck. Let's go do it. He was twenty six, not that big, very skinny. If I needed to, I could man-handle him out of my house. But, I could also just have some fun for a minute.

Back at the flat I was still flying high off the MDMA. I decided I needed a big glass of vodka. I poured myself essentially a quarter of a pint, with a dash of tonic water. I then proceeded to take another bomb of MDMA.

Everything that happened after that was all a bit blurry. I don't think he knew what hit him. That's the thing with MDMA, it just takes you out of all those negative thoughts you have. All your inhibitions go away. I know at some point I got my vibrator out; that makes me laugh. I can see his face now.

He was like, 'What is she doing?'

I had stopped all action and said, 'Wait a minute,' got my vibrator out and then said, 'Please continue.' The shy self that I usually am because I find it hard letting all my barriers down, especially when it is that exposed, had just all melted away.

The most fun was being had, that was for sure. He certainly wasn't trying to get himself into a unusual position to make me piss myself. He was pushing for sex without a condom on.

I said, 'No way, you get that bag on, naughty. I don't know where you have been. I certainly do not want to be catching anything or ending up pregnant!'

I am sure we ended up falling off the bed at one point. I don't need to tell you step by step what was happening. You can very well imagine what was going on. He was very attentive, that's all you need to know.

As my head cleared and I was more aware of what was happening, he sat on my big leather chair in my room and said, 'I have had the most amazing time, but please may I go home now?'

So funny, he asked permission to leave. He certainly did not ask me if I had an orgasm.

I was thoroughly disappointed, and tried to seduce him in to staying, but the fun time was up. Time to get back to reality. He said his goodbyes and that was the end of that. I did stalk him later on Facebook. He had posted a video clip of him playing his trumpet or clarinet or something of that type of instrument when he returned home. He felt the need to share his joy. Bless.

I feel it is a rite of passage to explore your sexuality when you leave a relationship, especially one that was so suppressive, abusive and wholly demeaning. You have to find yourself again. Be selfish, take what you want. Be kind, but one hundred percent own your emotions. Run with them. Feel them, embrace them. Do not make excuses about how you feel or why you feel. Trauma in any form, big or small, is going to take time to come out of you.

I did not cry once when I left Scott. But I was traumatised. I needed to just be free to deal with my demons in my own way, within the realms of moving forwards and not burying myself in drugs and alcohol to the point that I lost everything. I needed to have fun. I needed to feel free. I needed to just be me. The curious free spirit that I am at heart.

Off to Bristol it was. It was a Paul van Dyke night. A bit trancey but not too hard. I hate hard house music. It's like heavy metal. I hate heavy metal. It's just a bloody racket. Not my thing at all! We were going up by train on the night, partying hard, out of the club when it shut and straight on to the train home. The train ride was going to be two and half hours. It was going to be a tough journey home, but well worth the adventure out of town.

A bottle of Jägermeister for the journey up there and playing sherbet dib dab with the love drug to get us in the mood when we got there.

By the time we arrived we were well up for it. I was so happy and taking in every single minute of my freedom and being with my mates. We queued up and were told to go over to where the coats are handed in. I kept seeing signs for wearing helmets. I thought, 'That's weird.'

My mate was thinking the same thing. 'Why have we got to put helmets on?' It turns out the club was a skate park during the day, the signs were there for the skate park not for clubbing. We were all laughing, realising we were all now flying and hadn't got a clue what's going on.

Into the club we went. We arranged a point to meet in case we lost each other, and then it was off to the dance floor.

We danced and became best friends with random men and women just for those hours. I ended up on some guy's shoulders. A photographer at the event happened to capture it. I am forty-three, and some twenty-three-year-old has picked me up and I am loving life.

As I was wandering around the club at the end of the night, I pass by this young man. He said, 'OH my god, you are a MILF!'

I was about to tell him off, but then had to remember I was in amongst kids whom I was twenty years older than. I replied, 'Not a MILF, but a WILF! A woman you would like to fuck!' I laughed. He was cute. He wanted my number. I gave it to him, God knows why. It was the attention. Who doesn't love a bit of attention from a younger man? He said he was going to message me.

I said 'Sure,' and left it at that.

It was now six a.m. in the morning. My dancing feet were done. I wanted to go home. We made our way to the train station and had to wait an hour for the train to Bournemouth. I was bored and started to message the young guy. I think he was twenty-two. I was so bad. I mean, twenty-two. So young.

The train journey was arduous, but I felt like a rock star. I had my shades on, and I was messaging a twenty-two-year-old! How life had changed in such a short space of time. I was living life, and embracing every single part of it.

The messaging with the twenty-two-year-old went on all week. He was being very flirty, telling me all the things he was going to do to me. I, of course, did not stop this behaviour and let him run with it. He then messaged me to tell me he was on his way down to Bournemouth to see me.

At first, I was like, 'Shit! I didn't think this through.' I had spent the whole week winding him up sexually. He was now on his way to collect. What the fuck was I going to do with a twenty-two-year-old?

I told my friend who was living with me at the time that she had to come with me. We can take him into town, and she was not to leave my side.

I went and met him at the train station. As he got off the train, I thought, 'Holy fuck, he looks young.' I mean I was old enough to be his mum. I thought, 'Right Janine, don't be an asshole! This guy has taken the trouble to come and visit you. The least you can do is show him a good time.'

At one point of the night when we were sat in the bar, he had said he felt like a pimp. He was just relishing being out with us both and soaking it all up.

I showed him a good time, he left the next day, and all I need to say on the matter is that sex with a twenty-two-year-old is frantic; slow down was a key word in the whole experience. He left the next day. We spoke for a bit, but it was never going to go anywhere. The messaging just fizzled out. Time to focus and get back to study and training.

Finding Rafael

Scott's letter-writing was out of control. Reams and reems of paper, hand-written, which flowed between trying to be nice to me and then just being twisted with anger because I had left him. The owner of the martial arts gym I worked at approached me one day and asked me if it was OK for Scott to come back training. I mean, he was asking, but not really. The martial arts arena is still a boy's club and women are still working hard to find our position in that environment. I said, 'I don't really want him in the gym, but I also don't care.' It was so important to stay indifferent. If I showed any kind of emotion, it would show that I still cared. I did not care at all.

Scott was now back in the gym. He made a point of turning up and training in classes that ran alongside mine so that he was in the gym at the same time. I would ignore him. He would make a point of saying, 'Davis, Davis, Davis. Hello Davis.'

I would choose to ignore all of it, but on a couple of occasions I told him very sternly,' DO NOT FUCKING TALK TO ME!' Then I would just continue with my work like he did not exist.

I knew that it was driving him mad because he could not get to me.

One morning, after I had parked my car and was on my way to the gym, I was just about to cross the road and he appeared. He must have followed me down the road. He squared up to me. His eighteen-stone build to my eleven-stone build. His nasty curled up face in mine. I was just about to bite, but I managed to hold the words in and say nothing. I then had to go into the gym and teach my kids class with him in the boxing session that ran alongside mine.

I didn't tell anyone what was happening. I didn't want to make a fuss. I was getting second-hand information that he was really caning the vodka, cocaine and steroids at that time. When I got home from that morning, I realised that his behaviour was getting worse, and it was only a matter of time before he would do something to hurt me. I was scared; who did I have to protect me? No one!

'Right, I know what, I'll call the police for some advice.'

I spoke with a very nice lady over the phone, who reassured me that I had done the right thing by calling them. She told me that an officer would be out to see me that afternoon to discuss what was going on. I felt comforted and happy about the fact that I could at least see my options for being protected against an eighteen-stone alcoholic that was loaded with cocaine and steroids.

I waited in that afternoon, to then be contacted by the police that they were terribly sorry but an officer was not available and that one would come and see me the following day. I was disappointed, but thought, 'OK, I'll book out my afternoon from work and wait for the following day.'

The following day arrives. I receive another phone call, 'Ms Davis, we are terribly sorry, but no officer can see you this afternoon. We will send one this evening.' OK, I had booked out my afternoon from work, but OK. I'll wait for this evening. No one came!

I get a phone call the following day, the third day of waiting for an officer to come and talk to me about my ex-husband, whose behaviour was incredibly unpredictable. I genuinely was frightened for my life at that point. 'Ms Davis, we are so sorry. We will send someone this evening.' NO ONE TURNED UP.

FORTH DAY, THE SAME

FIFTH DAY, THE SAME

By this time, I was so enraged by the way they were treating me, that I phoned them and told them, 'I live right next door to the police station. I mean, it doesn't even take five minutes to come to my house. I will come to the station and see someone there!'

So, I went to the station on the sixth day, and I reported in the reception desk. I sat in my seat and they left me there for over an hour. As I sat there, I was now beyond the point of rage. I felt completely let down by the very people that I thought would be there as a last resort to protect me. I got out of my seat went home and phoned them and tore a new asshole into the woman over the phone. She profusely apologised, and promised me that someone would be at my house the following day.

I had now waited seven days for a police officer to visit my home. When the police officer arrived at my home, I explained what was happening, and told him how I felt. I showed him the letters that he did not even look at. He took one look at me (I'm five eight and eighty kilos, I do not look like a victim) and said, 'Well, you've left him. He's a bit upset!'

I knew then that I was on my own. I looked at that police officer and told him to get out of my house. I had to make a decision then. Do I live my life in fear, or do I just get busy living? Whatever happens is going to happen. That was the day I stopped being afraid. Fuck you Scott, and fuck you to the police. I was on my own.

I would say eighty percent of men that meet me want to

challenge me physically in some way or another.

'Show me your biceps.' 'Can we have an arm wrestle?' 'Can you pick me up above your head?'

Fucking idiots, that is their first school of thought. They expect me to perform like a dancing monkey, to stand there and flex my biceps because seeing a strong woman is a novelty. The touching does my head in as well. And why does arm wrestling signify power?

Anyway, I was out, and this guy had spotted me on the dance floor and made a bee line for me. He challenged me to pick him up. So, I went for it. I went to pick him up in a fireman's lift. Fuck him! I get so sick of telling these idiots to do one that I thought 'Right this time, I'll show him.' He shat himself. I suppose he thought I wasn't going to do it.

We got to talking and he decided that he was going to walk me home. When these guys find out that there is more to me than the outer layer, and that I have different depths to my personality, they are always intrigued to find out more.

I asked him in for tea. He didn't stay, but he took my number. We inevitably went out on a date. It turned out that he was a conspiracy theorist. It is quite draining being around people like that. I didn't really fancy him, but he wasn't a troglodyte. I asked him back to mine, and he ended up spending the night. Now, how does this happen? How can someone that is doing your head in a little bit, and who you do not really fancy, give you the best sex ever? I mean, I have enjoyed sex; not all the time, because some guys are just out for themselves. I can honestly say I have not had that many orgasms. But this guy, well, it was off the scale.

I did not want to be seen in public with him. I knew that there was a shelf life with this person, because at some point he was just going to start really doing my head in with all his theories.

187

The more time we spent together, the more the theories escalated. I did go out for dinner with him. I sat opposite him trying to find something that I could warm to. He did have nice eyes, but, no! It just wasn't enough. He had finished his meal and I was finishing up my mushroom stroganoff. He proceeded to get a tissue and blow his nose. Not such a bad thing, but after he had blown his nose, he proceeded to look at the tissue to see what he had blown out of his nose whilst I was still eating my dinner. It made my stomach turn.

'Are you for real? Are you really checking out your bogies whilst I am finishing my food?'

His reply, 'There isn't anything I wouldn't do in public.'

'Well, can you not do that whilst I am eating?'

That was the end of that, no, no, no… great sex over and out. Be gone with you.

My wild tendencies and wanting to just sleep with guys were kind of running their course. I really don't like one-night stands. They don't make me feel good about myself. Every time you have sex with someone as a one night stand it is like a little bit of your soul leaves when they leave. It's a short fix, that leaves an empty hole to fill once it is over.

Rafael was never too far away from my thoughts. One of the first things I had done when I left Scott was to email his friend Jose. He fortunately did get back to me, but he hadn't seen Rafael in a very long time. That was the end of that lead.

I was sat in my room, one Saturday afternoon in May of 2016, and decided to type his full name into google. I don't know why I hadn't done that before. A few hits come up. I clicked on a Facebook hit and there, to my surprise, was his picture. My heart literally skipped a beat. I had found him.

Being In My Love Bubble

Finding Rafael's picture, and feeling how my heart had started beating so fast, I knew then that I had never loved Scott. I sat there for a bit stalking Rafael's Facebook. Looking at pictures, trying to see if I could see how his life was right now. Was he still in San Fran? Was he married? Would he remember me? Should I call him? Shall I friend request him? What if he doesn't see the friend request? If I send him a message, that will go through to the friend request section and he may never see it. I've looked in my friend request section and sometimes you don't pick those messages up for over a year.

Well, it had been eighteen years, what did one more matter? I sent the message. 'Hi, it's Janine, do you remember me? Hope you are well; it would be lovely to hear from you x'

I couldn't believe that I had found him. My long-lost love. The love that I had always thought about. I got on with my day and tried not to think about it.

Memories are so funny. I was so caught up with how I felt about him and thinking about my feelings towards him, that I did not for one minute contemplate all the bad things he had done to me when I met him eighteen years before. I didn't think about how he had stood me up in Vegas when we were supposed to marry. How he used me, time and time again. In my delusion, I just wanted to find him and love him and for him to love me.

Five p.m., Saturday, 16 May 2016. I got a message. 'Of course I remember you! What's your number so that we can talk?'

I phoned him on the house phone to start with. I was so excited. I was telling him everything that I had achieved. I asked him if he was still in San Francisco.

'No, I am in Hawaii.'

He was working as a gardener. He then said, 'Right, how are we going to do this?'

That was it, we were together. I never questioned it. I was in. I asked him if he had messenger so that we could Facetime. He downloaded it and we called each other. We just looked at each other for a minute without saying a word. It was powerful. He was older, but I could still see him. The beautiful him that I had fallen in love with eighteen years ago. He asked, 'How are we going to see each other?'

'I don't know. I'm not allowed to visit the USA.'

He didn't have a passport. I said, 'Don't worry. I will figure this out.'

We chatted for a little while longer, he then said he had to get on, and that I was to call him when I woke up.

'OK.'

I had the biggest smile on my face, and my heart felt full to the brim. After I had finished the call, he had started to text me. He messaged, 'I have something I need to tell you. Shall I message you or phone you?'

'Just phone me.'

He called me back and told me he had HIV.

I wasn't surprised, but OK.

He said, 'I just thought you should know.'

'Thank you, I love you. I'll speak to you in the morning.'

There is still a lot of ignorance around HIV. I didn't bat an eyelid. I am not an ignorant person and I loved him. I would care

190

for him and stand by him through whatever he had. I can't understand people who walk away from people that are suffering.

A friend of mine the other day told me that her partner was not coping with the fact that she had cancer. I mean, what the actual fuck? He's not coping. What the fuck has he got to cope with? These weak fuckers, all you need to do is be there. Support, care, and just be a normal compassionate human being.

Rafael then sent me a song. 'Boz Scaggs, Loan Me a Dime.' I played it and played it and played it. Rafael finds it difficult to communicate and I felt that this was his way of communicating to me what he was feeling at that time.

My default is just wanting someone to love me. If I love them enough, they will love me back.

The following week was a whirlwind. There is an eleven-hour time difference between U.K and Hawaii. We spoke every morning and every night. I was one hundred percent in a love bubble. By the end of the week, we were getting married and I was going to have a child with him. This was my last chance to have a child with anyone. I was forty-four years old. If it was going to happen, it needed to be now. The clock was ticking.

Rafael had promised me that he had turned his life around, and that he had changed. I am too easy to give people the benefit of the doubt. I had to believe him. I had to give it this last chance, even if it was to put closure to something that I had thought about for the last eighteen years.

What I needed to do then was get divorced from Scott. I needed that to happen really fast.

I knew Scott was never going to divorce me. All that bullshit about getting my details back in 2015 to pursue the divorce was just a ruse to get my details and know where I was living. I did some research online, and found a company that did quicky divorces. We had no assets and no kids, so it should just be straight forwards. I was going to go with separation but, fortunately for me, I had a client at the time that was a family divorce solicitor. She advised me to go with unreasonable behaviour. I had told her a few bits from why I had left him. She suggested that if I did separation it would open up the lines of communication. He would be in control again. I would be in a place of begging him to sign the papers.

If I went with unreasonable behaviour, I would keep the control. I wouldn't have to speak to him and, if he refused to sign the papers, I could then pay for a court bailiff to make him sign.

It was going to cost me. But it was worth it. I needed to get this done quick smart. Rafael wanted to book an appointment at the town hall to get married, and I couldn't do that without my divorce being finalised.

I had to come up with six reasons as to why I wanted the divorce. It wasn't too difficult to come up with those reasons. My solicitor friend told me to send them to her, just to make sure I had the wording right. Once she had read them through, she suggested I take out the attempted murder. We were both laughing. I mean, you have to laugh. Of course, at the time you don't even realise what it is you are caught up in. Now I was out the other side I could laugh about it. She advised me that it could potentially make him mad that I had disclosed that, and also the police may want to speak to me.

The drinking, the lack of working, the women, the videos of his penis, the constant lying. Everything I put in those reasons was one hundred percent true. I did not lie about any of it.

What Scott didn't realise is that the papers would get sent back to me. He had decided to write his own comments on them. He wrote that I had shown unreasonable behaviour by not communicating, and that he was going to pay for the divorce, but because I did not communicate, he was not going to do that now. Fucking idiot.

My divorce was granted, of course. He didn't pay a penny. He apparently had said that I had assassinated his character.

It's funny; after the divorce, the shitting in my driveway stopped. The only person I could think of that would do something like that in broad daylight was him. For three years. Once a year in my driveway someone took the biggest dump. It was disgusting. I was also told that he still can't believe that I left him. The mind of the narcissist.

I was now one hundred percent free. I was officially Janine Davis.

My next mission now was getting my visa to the USA.

Mission Hawaii

The only way for me to get a visa to enter the USA was to make an appointment at the US embassy. I wasn't able to get an ESTA online because I answered yes to one of the questions they ask.

'Have you ever been a human trafficker?'

'Have you ever been a terrorist?"'

'Have you ever been a prostitute?'

'Have you ever sold guns?'

Whenever I look at those ESTA's, one would assume that those types of people are certainly not going to be answering 'Yes,' to any of them. Unfortunately for me, one of the questions asked is, 'Have you ever been stopped from entering the country?' Of course, I had. So that meant I had to ask permission to be let back in. This was now May 2016, and from the looks of things, the next available appointment was July 2016. It was in Northern Ireland. I couldn't get one in London, so Belfast was the next best option.

I booked my appointment, booked my flight, booked a hotel to stay in overnight and then just had to sit back and wait.

Me and Rafael were still talking every morning and every night. I would ask him, 'What about meeting in Mexico or Canada?'

He would nod his head, but not really come up with any solutions. It all fell on me.

I know, I know. The signs were there right from the beginning!

At that time, I didn't care, I was caught up with how I used to feel about him. I had found him and I wasn't going to let him go. July came around soon enough. I had a super smart outfit to make sure I looked the part. I wanted to make a good impression. A nice cream-coloured blouse, black wide-leg trousers that fitted super well round my hips and ass. No heels; I can't walk in heels. An open-toe black sandal with a little bit of a wedge. I felt good and professional. I was ready.

On the morning of the interview me and Raf spoke. He wished me good luck and told me to call him as soon as I got out of the meeting.

I can't tell you how anxious I was. I arrived really early to the appointment. I thought it would be a free-for-all. It was really civilised, and so many people were there with stories like mine. I did actually feel really overdressed. Most of them had just turned up in their jeans. I took my spot in the queue and waited to be called.

I got up to the counter with all my paperwork. I had collected references from work and friends to reaffirm my good character. I didn't need them. I was in there all of about five minutes. The lady was friendly. Asked me why I wanted to visit. I told her, 'I would like the opportunity to see my friends and family.'

She then said, 'Fine. This all happened such a long time ago. We will put you through the system and I imagine it will all be fine.'

That was that. I just had to sit back and wait. It wasn't a no, but it also wasn't a yes. I just had to wait. There was a backlog, so I would hear back in maybe around three months.

I felt positive.

Rafael had asked after my dad. I said, 'I don't talk to him.'

He suggested that I put everything aside and try to mend the

195

relationship. Rafael had become quite good friends with my dad when I was living in the USA. They had exchanged numbers and used to hang out together. I don't think Dad knew anything of Rafael's behaviour towards me back in the '90s. I don't think he would have even cared anyway. I didn't have that kind of relationship with my dad. Dad was happy hanging out taking drugs and getting high. He certainly wasn't in a place where he would advise me on relationships.

I reached out to my dad and told him that me and Rafael had re-connected, and were planning to marry. He responded to me and did the usual speech. I've always loved you, blah, blah, blah. So, the honeymoon period starts. He's phoning me. I get Leigh involved again because you think that this time it's going to be different. We were speaking quite a lot. It was nice. Of course it's nice. Your dad is interested in you for a moment. You feel wanted and loved just for a brief second.

Rafael even met up with my dad in San Francisco and asked if he could marry me. Rafael was going to be in San Francisco meeting up with family and suggested that my dad come by so that he could ask him. Dad was trucking through that way so I arranged the meet. I felt sad that I wasn't going to be there. Rafael was trying to do the right thing. I did get caught up in it all. No one had ever done that for me before. I mean really, my dad who had never been there ever, what did his opinion matter? But, that's what Raf wanted to do. No ring though, lets bear that in mind for a minute.

I'm not a materialistic person, I don't care about stuff like that. I didn't question it. It wasn't mentioned. I was too busy trying to figure out how I was going to meet up with Rafael. I did push him on his passport again. Nothing. I still to this day do not know why he does not have his passport. He certainly wasn't

196

going to do anything about getting it, that was for sure.

It was now November 2016, and I checked my email every day to hear whether or not my visa had been granted. I had decided to do a day out in London on my birthday. I had gone with my mate Grace. We had lunch in a really posh restaurant, round the corner from the Natural History Museum. The lunch had cost around £50. I only had a cup of tea and a plate of pasta. I mean, it was nice, but really, £50. But it was my birthday and I didn't care. We hit up the Natural History Museum. The dinosaurs were cool, the rest of it was 'meh.' The funniest part of the museum was the funny mirrors you normally find in a fairground. Grace had had a smoke (weed), so I had probably had a bit of a passive hit. We laughed so hard at us two in those mirrors. I'm five foot eight and stacked, and Grace was just hitting five foot and tiny. The way the mirrors distorted us both was just hilarious. We were in there for ages. People that were looking around the museum were starting to look in at us, to see what we were laughing so hard at.

We left the museum, passed Harrods, and wanted to check out the Christmas lights down Oxford Street. We had a look in Liberty. Oh my god, that building is beautiful, and inside is just as breath-taking. I then bought some woolly gloves from Ralph Lauren for £50! We made our way to the train station to come back to Bournemouth. A good day was had, and I was feeling very content. I sat on the train as we were leaving Waterloo and checked my emails. It had come. They had granted me the Visa. I was to send to my passport for it to be issued. I was now allowed to go back to the USA. What a day!

Over the years of being banned from the USA, I had so many recurring dreams about getting out there. They were all so weird, and in my dreams, I would never quite make it.

This was all about to change.

All I had to do now was book my flights and get myself out there.

My story was a fairy tale story. Everyone was so happy for me. Old love found again. I was moving to Hawaii, getting married and trying for a child. This was my last attempt at having a child. Being forty-four meant the clock was ticking really fast if this is what I wanted.

My flight was booked for 9th February 2017. It was the cheapest time to fly to San Fran. It was also just before Rafael's birthday, which fell on 13th Feb. I thought it would be a good idea to be there for his day.

Let's get one thing straight: I was totally, one-hundred-percent invested in starting a life with Rafael. I was ready to uproot myself and move to another country to start a different life. But I was also clear headed enough to go on this trip to find out who he really was. Had he changed? Was he a better person than when I had met him in the '90s? I hadn't just come out of an eleven-year relationship with an abusive alcoholic to jump straight back into another one. Really, at this point I was so caught up in the romance of it all and going to Hawaii that I did not think for one minute that I was going into anything bad. I just needed to go and see. Find out who he was as an adult. I was eighteen years older. I wasn't that completely insecure young girl that he had met in the '90s. I had grown up. I had unresolved emotions that I need to put closure to with Rafael.

I had arranged to spend a day or so with my dad. He was going to meet me at the airport, which was cool. I was also talking to my sister around this time. I believe she was pregnant with her fourth child.

Travelling is so exciting. Right from the moment you leave

your house with your bags packed. New places, new faces, new experiences. I was going to Hawaii; I couldn't believe it. I had decided to fly to Oakland. Number one, it was cheaper than San Francisco Airport, and number two, I had PTSD from San Francisco Airport. I was terrified of being pulled again at customs and not being allowed to go through again.

Going through customs in Oakland came with its own issues, though. My heart was pounding out of my chest when I was waiting in line. I was next to go up to the officer. I had tried to have a word with myself. It was like I was going into the ring. Thank goodness I am fit. I am sure it was beating at max rate before I went up. He asked me all the usual questions. What was the purpose of my visit? How long was I staying? Where will I be staying? I told him I was visiting my dad. If I told him I was visiting Rafael and was looking to get married, he would never have let me through.

The visa in my passport was a special visa, meaning I was told to go and sit in the chairs at the back of the customs place and wait for an officer to come and speak to me. I thought, 'Here we go again.' I messaged my dad. I said, 'I'm not getting in.'

Jokingly, he said, 'OK, there's a bus you can catch if you make it through. I'll catch you later.'

At the time I was not in a place for fucking about and jokes. I was highly stressed. Idiot. He then said, 'Don't worry, you'll be fine.'

The customs officer took me in a room and started to ask me questions about my visit. For every one of his questions, I answered with a question of my own. I was panicking. I then thought, 'What the fuck are you doing, just tell the truth!'

I said, 'Look, I was an idiot, eighteen years ago. I fucked up. I have done my time and turned my life around. I would just like the opportunity to visit my friends and family again.'

He sat there for a moment and said, 'OK.' He stamped my passport and I was free to go and get my bags. I couldn't believe it. I was out the other side. I had made it!

Dad was outside the airport. We were on our way to San Miguel, where he now lived. It's a really small town, south of San Jose. It was like stepping into an old western town from the cowboys and American Indian era.

Being with Dad was cool. It always is in the beginning. It's the honeymoon period. The time when the act can stay intact. I realise now, that he could only spend a short amount of time with me. A good couple of days, and then time for him to get back to trucking. Dad was back to his lorry driving all over America. He would be away for at least a month and then come home for a weekend, before he was back out on the road again. I had timed it so that it was his weekend to have off. That way when he was setting off, he could drop me back to the airport, so that I could fly out to Hawaii.

Sarah was pleasant. She was always pleasant. She could also hold an act that meant she could care enough for me to be around for a short amount of time before she had had enough.

I had stepped into the CrossFit world just before my journey. I had, on a whim, entered a friendly comp at the gym in Bournemouth while I was working. I came second. I didn't have a clue what I was doing, but I had got the bug. It was intense. It was a fitness I hadn't felt since my Thai boxing days. I knew I needed to get fitter and CrossFit ticked a lot of boxes for me. Lifting, cardio, and something super new for me: gymnastics. I was forty-four years old and I was learning how to handstand walk and do ring muscle-ups. It was fab.

Sarah had said that she had started CrossFit and I was

welcome to come to the gym she went to. I jumped all over that. When we arrived at the CrossFit box, Sarah introduced me as her stepdaughter. I looked at her out of the corner of my eyes. 'When have I ever been your step daughter?' I thought. She then introduced me as a world champion. I thought, 'You bitch. Yeah, I see what's going down. I have now earnt some credits as an individual that she wants to be associated to, as the world champ. So, she'll introduce me as her stepdaughter.' People are weird. I let her get on with it. I hadn't seen her in eighteen years and now I was her step daughter. Go figure.

The time flew past. Like I said, it was nice, but what could really go wrong in two days? Dad was playing his part. He would always ask me questions about Mum. I have lost count of the number of times I have told him I don't like her. Me and Leigh have nothing to do with her.

He would then re-tell stories of how they met. How my nan, my mum's mum was cruel. How Grandad Tom, my mum's dad, became an alcoholic because of my mum and my nan. He told my dad that he was crazy for marrying my mum. He would often repeat how beautiful she was. I mean, I suppose it's nice to hear that at least they were in love when I was conceived, and that at one point they liked each other. He also told me that Mum had had an affair, and that was why he left. But, he has never ever taken responsibility for the fact that he relinquished his role as a parent to me and Leigh. I don't think he ever sees us as his children, or ever has. He had, at some point in the 70s, exonerated himself from all parental responsibility. I'm sure he would have done the same with Ashley, my sister, but Ashley's mum was on it and didn't let him get away with it. They are a bit tougher in the USA with child support. He thought by leaving California he would get away with it. But he didn't, so he had to pay up.

GOOD!

I was now at Oakland airport. But, this time I didn't have to go through customs. This flight was like catching a bus. All I had to do was show my I.D, and I was on my way to Hawaii.

I was super nervous, excited, and above all, I could not believe I was in the USA.

Honolulu airport is pretty big. I had to walk miles to get my bags. I had messaged Rafael that I had landed. I was really apprehensive. I looked for him in the airport. I couldn't see him. The bags took forever to come out. Now I was outside the airport still looking for Rafael. Finally, this big white truck pulled up, he got out, and we hugged; it was awkward. On reflection, he was cold. The hug was not full of emotion. He was ticking boxes. I was so nervous. He didn't really make me feel relaxed. He then put a beautiful Lei around my neck and that was that. I got in the truck. I was just staring at him, just trying to take it all in. He then held my hand.

He said, 'I have just one more job to do. Do you mind if we go do that and then we'll head home?'

Me being me, I said, 'Sure.'

Even though I was knackered, hungry and could have done with just chilling out for a minute. Contrary to popular belief, I am a pretty easy-going person. I didn't kick up a fuss. I didn't want to be a pain, so I just went along with it. Whilst I have a voice most of the time, I am too busy thinking about everyone else, instead of thinking about my own needs.

Off we went. Rafael had a sprinkler system to tinker with. The garden that he was working in backed straight out on to Kailua beach. The bluest of blue sky, white sand as far as the eye could see, and volcanic mountains everywhere. Hawaii is breathtaking, and there I was after eighteen years of purgatory. I was standing on a Hawaiian beach, soaking in that blazing tropical sun, having to pinch myself that I was there and that I had found him.

Rafael finished his work and we headed back to his apartment. He had mentioned that his place was untidy.

I said, 'Not to worry.' I thought to myself, 'How bad could it be?' Well, let me tell you how bad it was. As soon as I walked through the door, I started to laugh. The shit that was everywhere was overwhelming. The dust was thick. Untidy was an understatement. I mean, he had had close to a year to get ready for me coming over. I looked at the bed; he had managed to wash the sheets. They were not on the bed, but they were clean at least. I said, 'I need the toilet.' I was praying that the bathroom was going to be clean. Had the bathroom not been clean, that would have been a deal breaker right there and then. Lucky for me, it was clean. Well, the toilet was clean. I thought, 'OK, I can work with this.' When he went out to work, I could clean the dust off, put the hoover round and try and put some order to the shit that was everywhere.

Once I had come out of the bathroom, there was no time to settle, talk, chill, eat. Rafael was straight into the shower. He barked some orders at me. We were now both in the shower. There was no tenderness, no caring. He did not think for one minute about how far I had come. That I might be knackered from all the travelling. His manner was cold, awkward and abrupt. It did not make me feel good, secure or loved. He barked at me about washing him down. I looked at him and thought, 'Fuck what have I got myself into now?' I stepped out of the shower, dried myself off and went and sat on the bed 'Fuck me, I've got three weeks of this to go.'

Rafael got himself out of the shower and came and sat with

me. I think that maybe he realised that his behaviour was a bit off, or that I was a bit off. His manner changed. We had sex, but it wasn't great. I realise that now. He does not know how to be intimate at all! He thinks because his dick is big, that's it. Get hard, stick it in. Not one clue about foreplay. I thought I loved him though. I went along with his bad behaviour. I was wishing for this to work. Maybe it was just first-time awkwardness. It could get better, right? I think he was used to women just doing what he wanted to do and that he could speak to them how he wanted. I realise now I don't know how to be loved. I don't know the difference between right and wrong.

After sex, I had wanted to talk about the past at least a little bit. There was stuff I needed closure to. He did not at any point want to engage in that. He point-blank refused to talk about the past. So, that was that. It was my first day there. I did not want to pursue it at that moment. I would give him some time to chill with me and I may well venture there again.

My default again: I was thinking about his feelings. Not pushing him. Letting him feel comfortable. Of course, he didn't want to talk about the past. It would mean opening up a can of worms he was not yet ready to deal with.

I think because of the medication he was on for his HIV and the fact that he had been a meth addict for fifteen years had meant that his libido was not what it was when he was in his twenties. I knew that he was having trouble with his erections. It didn't matter to me. I didn't bring it up. I thought 'I'll give him some space to talk about it when he's ready.' He kept mentioning about having more sex, so it was on his mind.

I told him not to worry. There was more to spending time together especially now that we were both twenty years older than just having sex. I mean, when you are totally into someone, who doesn't love it? But I loved him and was just happy to be there with him, sharing time and hanging out.

Rafael had got under my skin from the very first moment I had met him in 1996. My friend Cassandra called it the 'Rafael Spell.' It didn't matter what he did to me; I would still go back every time. Unfortunately for me, I just don't understand the difference between right and wrong when it comes to love. I don't know how to be loved. I grew up in dysfunction, which means I end up in dysfunction. I know how to love. I give an abundance of love, in the hope that they will love me back the same. I dismissed all the bad behaviour first time round and only remembered how I felt about him. I wanted desperately for it to work. I had found him. The first trip, I was in romance land. Rafael wanted to marry me again, he wanted to have a child with me. This was my last chance. I could put up with the odd bit of baggage here and there.

I was in a place of ignoring all the signs that were right in front of me. I was still in a place where I was desperate to find someone, anyone to love me.

After the first day, I settled in. I had taken my studying with me. It was a good opportunity to really concentrate on getting my master's finished. I found a CrossFit gym to go to. I had ventured down to twenty-four hour Fitness. Some super-nice guy was reeling me in and trying to get me to sign up and pay a monthly subscription. I stopped him in his sales track and said, 'Buddy, how much is this going to cost me?'

'$150, and if we get you signed up, it is only going to cost you x amount for when you come back.'

I was like, 'Dude, how much is a single entry going to cost me?'

'$15.'

Right, that is what it will be. Bloody $150, who was he trying to kid? Those places. Honestly, if you are not sharp, they will pull you in, and before you know it, you are signing all your money away!

I then found CrossFit Kailua, the dude there was super friendly. He said 'Bung me $25 and that will be fine for the three weeks you are here.'

So that was that. I certainly wasn't paying $150. Whilst Rafael was at work, I could go to the CrossFit, get back to do my study, have a little mooch about while I wait for him to get back from work and then we could hang out.

Rafael was drinking a lot. Coming out of a relationship with someone that was an alcoholic. I did not want to repeat this type of behaviour. It was nothing for Rafael to start drinking in the day, while he was driving me around. Six to eight bottles a day. I mean, you can argue the fact that American beer is like drinking piss, but none the less, I did not want to be with someone that was drinking that much.

I bought it up in conversation one night. Tried to open the conversation that was not attacking but more of an observation. He took it well. We had a discussion and the following day he told me that he wasn't going to drink any more. The first trip was like that. He had brief interludes of being caring and thoughtful. He wanted to please me. In day-to-day stuff. Whilst I could talk to him about his drinking and not hitting his dog, the intimacy never improved. I loved him though, so I went along with what he offered with the hope that we would be able to be in a place where we could talk about it. He didn't have a fucking clue. It was all on his terms. not at any time did he think about what my desires were, or how to please me on any level. Get hard, stick it in, that was about it. For me to open up I need to feel safe, secure.

I need to know that the person that is with me is one hundred percent not going to hurt me. Even though I loved him, I held back. Let me tell you something: I do not go around sticking every man's penis in my mouth on a whim. I mean, all this preoccupation with anal fucking means that most of the dicks out there have been up some person's shitter! Fact! Why on earth would I want to put something in my mouth that has potentially been up some person's ass! He berated me for that. Made fun of me, made me feel bad. I did not care. I am comfortable saying 'No,' and meaning it, until I am ready to make that choice for myself. I will not be made to feel bad or coerced into doing something just because I am afraid of what that other person thinks of me. So, I am a prude. I don't fucking care. They are just words, and my self-respect and dignity mean more than doing something for someone just because they want it!

You will have to be a really fucking special person for me to do that. You will certainly have to put in some ground work for that special nugget to come out of the trick bag. You cunts out there that think it's funny to hold the back of a woman's head and ram you dick down our throats are out of your fucking mind. So, fuck you. I will do it when I am good and ready to do it, and not when you are waving your dick around in my face.

Thankfully for me, Rafael's dick was broken, so fortunately there wasn't that much of that going on.

Sight-seeing while I was there wasn't much of a priority. I thought I was moving there, so I didn't have a sense of urgency to go see stuff. Rafael did take me to a view point where you could see the Honolulu city. Raf had a beat-up old vintage car that he was fixing up. He decided it would be a good idea to take it for a ride to see Chinaman's hat, a very tiny island off the beach coast that looks like a Chinaman's hat. It was miles from his home, and the 1972 Volkswagen nearly didn't make it back. The last adventure was driving up to the North Shore. Thankfully, we didn't go in the Volkswagen. We stopped off at a coffee farm, and I saw miles and miles of pineapples growing out of the ground. I didn't know that pineapples grew out of the ground. That was about it, really. I never did get to go surfing there, which is something I wanted to do. I thought I had all the time in the world to do it because I was going to be living there.

He had a little dog called Paco. Paco was a Chihuahua. Chihuahuas like to bark a lot. I watched him hit the dog on numerous occasions. I told him to stop it, get a little spray bottle of water rather than hitting him. He did try to stop that behaviour while I was there on the first trip and went for shaking his keys. I'm not sure why. He said that the dog was scared of them. I thought, 'As long as he was not hitting him, fine.'

There were nuggets of bad behaviour slipping through. I went with him one day to help him with his work. I was sweeping up the leaves. Does it matter which way you sweep them? I went down to the bottom of the leave pile and decided to sweep towards the bin.

Raf shouted at me, 'Woman! What are you doing?'

Startled, I looked at him and told him what I was doing. He then wanted me to do it his way. I mean, it made no difference at all. It's just sweeping leaves, right? Why did it matter so much which way I was sweeping them. I let him have his control though, and swept the way he wanted me to do it.

He also had loads of empty plastic bottles in the back of his truck strewn about. I started to clean them up, but he angrily told me to just leave them alone. I thought to myself, 'He's getting his knickers in a twist over nothing. I'm only trying to help.'

I got my period whilst I was there. I was in quite a bit of pain and he wanted me to go with him to pick some flowers for a garden he was doing. I said, 'Sure,' even though I just wanted to lay down and do nothing.

It was quite nice at the garden centre. Garden centres are really peaceful. We chose the flowers together and decided to make our way back to his flat.

We pulled up at a junction and he decided to throw a bottle into the back of his truck. The bottle missed the back and landed in the road. He then jumped out of the truck at the junction to get the bottle because he didn't want to litter. He did not leave the truck in park. The truck started to roll back. I did not have time to pull on the hand brake because I had all the plants over my lap. The truck was massive. The car behind, not so much. It smashed in the front of the vehicle.

That was the end of that day. After they had exchanged details. His way of dealing with it was to get shit-faced. So weird and weak, if you ask me. I mean, it was only a little dent, no one died. He bought quite a few beers and went back to his place, where he decided to down the bottles. As we sat in the garden, whilst he was getting wrecked, out of the blue he said, 'You don't fancy taking it up the ass?'

I sighed, looked at him and thought 'What a piece of shit. How does that make me feel? Loved, cared for?'

I said, 'Really, with my tampon string hanging out and the fact I feel like utter dog shit? I'll give that one a dodge, if that's OK?'

He then went and passed out until the following day, where he woke up like nothing had happened. I was left to please myself, feed myself and just stay in the apartment with him flat out.

There was a real issue with the toilet as well. He brought up one day that I was peeing on the underside of the toilet seat. It took me by surprise really. I had never in my forty-four years ever been brought up about peeing on the underside of the toilet seat. I mean, it was the fucking toilet. I am not a dirty person. His excuse was that it leaves the toilet seat yellow. My toilet seats have never been yellow, because I clean my toilet regularly. I thought 'OK, that's weird. But I am in someone else's house, so every time I go to the toilet, I will pick up the seat and check it to make sure there is not the odd drop of pee on it.'

He also made a point of bleaching the bath every time I got out of it. It was starting to make me question myself. He complained about my small bit of hair down the plug hole. I have really long hair. That is going to happen when you shower. But like I have said before, I am a clean person. I may not get the hair out every day but I do clean regularly. So, that was another job to do to make sure I wasn't offending him.

I would understand if the rest of the place was spotless, but it wasn't! His shit, tools, clothes, shoes, general junk, thick dust, was EVERYWHERE!

I played ball though. I was caught up with the romanticism of being in Hawaii with a guy that I had longed for for eighteen years. It's funny what your memory does. I was connected to how I felt about him in my twenties and what he meant to me, but not to any of the bad behaviour I may have experienced eighteen years before that.

Really, all of those behaviours were warning signs, but I was still invested in making it work. I still loved him, and I was going to do my best to get myself out to the USA and start a life with him.

I am not a materialistic person, so the fact that he had asked me to marry him and hadn't gotten me a ring didn't bother me.

He bought it up when we were out driving one day. I said, 'I'm not bothered.' But after that conversation, we were in a gun shop. For me from the U.K, it seemed completely unbelievable that you could go to the end of your street and buy an assault rifle. He was looking to buy a gun that was over $800. But he couldn't get me a ring. Go figure.

My worst trait is not seeing the bad behaviour signs soon enough.

I didn't question the gun-buying incident because I loved him, so I brushed it aside. I mean, I was in Hawaii with my long-lost love.

Towards the end of the trip, I was trying to get the visa paperwork together. I knew in my heart then that it was never going to work. Rafael didn't have a clue about that either. Rafael had never left the country. He didn't have a clue about going through customs. He thought I could tell them that I was coming to see my fiancé. I kept telling him that if I told them that, they would never let me through. Especially with my past track record. Both of us needed to have substantial amount of money in the bank. Neither one of us had that. I was willing to be patient and do a few trips and figure this stuff out. Rafael was super impatient and wanted me in Hawaii yesterday. He was not in a place where he was going to help with the paperwork either. It all fell on me.

I cried all the way home. I felt like he was just starting to open up to me and then I had to leave. He had opened up about his HIV. The weird thing was when he was opening up about his diagnosis, I realised I had dreamt about him in 2002 at the same time of his diagnosis. The dream was so real and clear, like he was right there with me. I reminded him of that dream when I was in Hawaii. He said there were a few people he was close to

211

who had had the same experience. He told me that he was in denial initially about the HIV, and thought that God was going to come and take it away for him. He actually ended up with full-blown AIDS. His viral load was at a million. The fact that he is still alive is truly amazing, really. He realised God wasn't going to save him, and he wanted to stay alive. The medication they have available for HIV enables people that are living with the virus to go on and have a full and long life. It certainly is not a death sentence any more.

He talked about his abuse as a small child. I think he had forgotten that I already knew about this. I just gave him space, and listened when he was ready to talk.

In my delusion, I thought, 'If we had just another couple of weeks, I think we would be in a better place. He would have opened up more and been able to talk about everything that he was holding up inside.'

My default is to love and care. I miss all the bad behaviour because I have never experienced the good.

Mission Hawaii, Part Two

After returning to the U.K., I was desperate to get back out there and spend more time with him.

You may ask, 'Why?'

I loved him, plain and simple. Love is weird. I suppose it can be like a sickness especially with the wrong person. Everyone around you can see what is happening, but you are so blind and so caught up with wanting this relationship to work, that you are ignorant to the bad behaviour.

I got my shit together, borrowed some money and got myself back to Hawaii in a twelve-week turn-around. I was taking another three weeks off work.

I am self-employed. I don't work, I don't get paid. Rafael was still no closer to getting a passport and coming to the U.K.

Back home I was downsizing and getting myself ready for the move. The first trip I had bought clothes with me to leave. I had done the same on the second trip. I would have been happy to just take the intensity out of the relationship, just take a bit of time getting to know one another again. He didn't want that. All or nothing. I didn't speak up and went along with what he wanted.

Whilst I was committed to making it work and caught up in the romance of it all, I was still not giving up everything here in the U.K. I knew deep down I was still working him out. I knew that at some point he may well disappear, as he always used to do back when we were together in the '90s.

I didn't stay with Dad this time. I spent the night with Rafael's mum, who lived in Pleasanton, about a twenty-minute ride from Oakland airport. I got hauled into the customs office again. Because of the type of Visa I have in my passport, US customs are always going to question me. Fortunately for me, I had the same officer as before. He recognised me, and said, 'Back so soon?'

'I had some time off so why not.'

I still did not make any reference to the fact I was out there visiting a guy I was potentially looking to marry. The officer stamped my passport, and I was on my way again. This was just a quick turnaround, just one night at Rafael's mum's and then on to my flight the following day to Hawaii.

Rafael's mum was nice, and we got a bite to eat. She then started to off-load information about Rafael. Most of it I knew, but I didn't know that his boys were six months apart. I had thought for some reason they were years apart. It started me thinking back to when I met him. I knew he had a whole other life or even lives going on. That's why he would disappear. I'm not sure how many women he had on the go at any one point, or even men. He was bisexual. That didn't bother me. To be honest I'm not bothered by much. If I like the person then I like them; there is never any judgement on my part. But his boys only being six months apart just started to open up my thinking process to who he was as a person. I mean, if we were going to have a child, why would his behaviour be so different now? I knew he did not have a hand in doing anything for those boys. I knew after I left San Francisco in 1996 his life was lived on the streets, taking meth for fifteen years.

He had promised me in 2016 that he was doing his best to live a life that was cleaner and more productive. The first trip

214

certainly showed a small inclination that he was clean.

The second trip was a different experience all together.

When he picked me up from the airport, he did not come and meet me, again. He was cold in the ride back to the apartment. I was super knackered from the travelling. Again, he had to finish a job. I had to trail along with him again. The apartment was just a shit pit as per usual. He did not take any time off work to spend with me. Just a couple of days would have been nice.

He was right back to hitting the dog; this behaviour had really accelerated. At one point I got hold of the dog to get between him, an eighty-kilo man and a tiny chihuahua, to stop him from hitting him. He stood over me and the dog and said to the dog, 'She's not going to be able to save you every time!'

One morning before he went off to work, he had taken a call from I think a cousin. I was sat on the sofa and he was sat on the floor in front of me. I could hear everything he was saying.

'Yeah cuz, I'm all good, just hanging... Yeah, yeah you know, just dropping some seed.'

I thought, 'What the fuck is he talking about? He can't be talking about me. I thought, seed, work, yeah, he must be talking about work.'

No, no, he was talking about me. He was talking about dropping his seed in me. Like it was nothing. Like I was nothing. I mean, if he was talking about me like that in front of me, what the fuck was he saying when I wasn't there? He disappeared into the kitchen. When he came back, I told him, 'I never want you to talk about me in that manner again. I am not a piece of meat. I am someone that you are wanting to marry. I am an intelligent, powerful woman. You will treat me with respect!'

He was shocked, didn't see that he had done anything wrong and went off to work. I then got a message to apologise for his

215

behaviour. He was fifty going on sixteen. I was dealing with a man-child.

He came home from work a couple of nights after that, and was in the bathroom fully naked. He had a massive hard on. He looked at me and said, 'You know what comes next!' No warm up, no telling me that I'm beautiful, no foreplay whatsoever. Just get hard and stick it in. This time though, he hurt me. I mean, my vagina was in its forties. My vagina was not twenty years old any more. It needed some kind of lubricant. But I was subservient, and he took what he needed. DROPPED HIS SEED... He then told me that I hurt him.

I said 'What, me?'

'You have fucking broken it.'

'My vagina has just been ragged by you and I hurt you?'

I bled for three days after that. He had torn it to pieces. I told him, 'You see this here,' as I pointed at my vagina, 'You see this? This is broke! You broke it, this area here needs warming up!'

He looked at me sheepishly, 'OK, we'll take it slow.'

Take it slow? Motherfucker, you need to go back to foreplay one 'o' one or foreplay for dummies!

The nit picking was still continuing, and starting to accelerate. I was wiping the toilet, bleaching the bath every time I got out of it. Apparently, I wasn't grinding his coffee beans enough, every morning. He also pulled out the coffee bean bag from the fridge and told me that it had to be folded over twice. I wasn't allowed to put the tea bags in the bin. So, I then took to putting each tea bag in the outside bin. When asked where I was going? I told him, 'Out to the bin with my tea bag!'

I had taken a poo, like we all take poo's. He had gone in the toilet after me. On his return his comment 'I forget you women shit!' Shut the door in future, it's disgusting! I was totally gobsmacked. Never mind the fact I had to listen to him farting and shitting every morning at four a.m.! In fact, the farting was unbearable. It was all the fucking time. The sound his ass made was like he was ripping himself a new fucking asshole every time. ALL DAY LONG. I didn't care. I don't judge. But, him on the other hand, God forbid that I should empty my bowels or even fart for that matter!

. When we went out, I let him pay for everything. Why the fuck not? I had spent a hell of a lot of money to get myself out there to Hawaii, TWICE.

Oh, and I didn't suck his dick. So fucking what?

It was getting to a place where I didn't want to go back to the apartment. I was not having a good time. I was on the other side of the world, on my own going, through hell.

There was a woman staying in the front of the house, visiting a friend. It turned out that she was a best friend of a woman that Rafael used to date back from San Francisco in the '90s. I mean, the chances of that happening are very slim. I think the universe planted her there and I was meant to meet her.

Rafael came home one day before lunch and said, 'Do you want to come and have some lunch with me and my work mate?'

'Sure.'

I had been studying hard, and the break would be nice. Off we went to this sports bar he liked to go to. I watched them both down four pints of lager.

I thought, 'Christ! that is not going to set you up so well for working this afternoon.'

He then, as we were sat there in the sports bar, told me about Maria, who was the friend of this woman that was staying at the front of the house we were living in. Apparently, he was meant to marry Maria at the same time as me in the 90s. I looked at him stunned; I then told him he was a fucking asshole! Why would he tell me that?

It was like the floodgates opening. I thought to myself, 'What the fuck are you doing? This fucking asshole has always been an asshole.'

All the feelings that I felt back in my twenties when he used to fuck me about all the time all came flooding back. It was then that I really started to question what my life would be like if I moved to Hawaii to live with him.

We left the sports bar and went back to the apartment. He then proceeded to have two bong hits with his work assistant and go back to work.

'Good luck this afternoon. I can't imagine you'll get much done, you fucking idiots!'

I took off down the beach for the afternoon to figure my head out and what I was doing. It just so happened that the woman turned up down the beach. She said, 'Hi, is Rafael in the water?'

'No, I'm on my own.'

'Oh cool, I'll sit with you.'

She was the first one to bring up the fact that Rafael had dated her best friend Maria when they both lived back in San Francisco. She had said that she was so happy that Maria had not stayed with him. I told her I knew him from back in San Fran and that he was probably dating us at the same time. I then told her that he would disappear all the time, without a word and then just reappear like nothing had happened. She said, 'Yes, he used to do that to Maria as well.'

She then told me that Maria was long shot of him and that she had a beautiful daughter now with a really lovely man. I think that maybe then she thought she had said too much. I said that we were planning to marry and try for a child.

218

She smiled. 'Well he is probably a bit more grown up now.' She thought that we would have lovely children.

The whole conversation left me perplexed. This trip was not good. His behaviour was not good.

When he returned home after getting wasted at lunch time, he spent a good hour complaining about the fact that his work assistant couldn't perform. I mean, what the actual fuck! You down four pints of lager and had two hits on the bong, what the fuck did you expect?

I did point that out. He did not see that at all. He expected more, stupid ass!

He mentioned to me one morning that I 'Just haven't stopped. With the gym that is.'

He was a personal trainer when I met him. He was in fine shape, that was for sure. I had only just started working out when we met in 1996. I had gone on to achieve great things with my sport. He had become a meth addict and thrown his life down the toilet. I think there was some resentment with that from him.

I soon realised as well that I was moving around the flat on egg shells. I stopped what I was doing and thought, 'Hang on a minute. This is not me, what the fuck am I doing?' This was all his shit; it was all his insecurities. He was projecting his shit on to me.

I was stood in the kitchen as he pulled up outside from work. I had been there two weeks by now. It was pretty horrendous at this point. I watched him get out of his truck and just stand by it. I had spent that day wandering around on my own again. He was struggling with his work load, and blamed me, really. I think he thought I should have been out with him, helping him. Which I would have, had he been able to communicate how he was feeling. But he was completely incapable of that.

I knew watching him from the window that I was in for it. He came into the apartment and just ignored me. I tried to make conversation with him, but he wasn't having it.

I said, 'Right, what the hell is wrong? If you have got something you want to say, get it out. Tell me what the fuck is wrong!'

But no. I was to sit and wait until he was ready to talk. I thought, 'Fuck this! I am not sitting like a naughty child waiting for him to talk to me. I have done nothing wrong.' I got my shit together and took myself out for dinner. I thought the space would clear the air a bit. I went back to the apartment after dinner, but he was gone. I thought maybe he had come out to find me. Oh, no. He saw that I was online. He messaged me to say, 'I hope you got what you needed,' and then bid me goodnight.

He left me on my own for the whole night. Not a word to say where he was, where he was staying. I have travelled half way around the world for him. I was uprooting my life to come and live with him, only for him to treat me this way. I was devastated. I thought, 'Fuck this shit!' He came back in the morning. Walked in the door with a right face on him. No 'Sorry.' No 'Let's talk.' He just threw himself on the bed and continued to sulk. I got myself up, pulled down my suitcase, packed all my shit up. Went into the garden and booked the first flight out of there to San Fran.

I phoned my dad, asked if I could stay there for a week and fucking left his sorry ass!

Rafael blocked me from everything. He wasn't open to any discussion what so ever. I suppose rightly so. But I was so rageful and emotionally traumatised. I didn't know where to direct my anger. When I arrived at my dad's, Dad was away working. I was staying with the wife, Sarah. Dad would be home at the weekend.

I locked myself away in my room and settled into to watching Netflix and laying out in the sun for a week. I wrote an extensive rageful email to Rafael because that was my only means of contact. His response to the email was. 'I am not going to bother myself with the content of this email. Good Bye!'

I had made a stand. I had left him. But there was nothing from him. I'm not sure what I was looking for. For him to say, 'I'm sorry. Please don't leave me. I love you.'

Dad came back on the weekend. He took us for a walk over some beach near him. He then took me to see the mission that is in the town. It was cool. I like looking at old shit. He could just about manage to spend at least a couple of days with me.

When he returned to work, I planned to catch a ride with him. San Miguel is three hours from San Fran. The trains were not that regular and there was no other way that I was going to get to Oakland airport. A few tears in the car, where he told me, to stop crying and 'Be tough like your Dad.'

I mean, what?

Tough like you? Are you fucking kidding? That man has no idea what tough is. All I needed at that point was a touch of compassion. Not to be shut down and told to be more like him!

He dropped me off at the airport, and we said our goodbyes. I had asked him if he would come to my graduation. He said, 'Sure.'

I then sat for ten hours waiting for my flight home. My period had arrived the day before as well. I was in hell.

Although I was distraught about leaving Rafael, I did realise that I had done the right thing. I had empowered myself out of a situation I was getting into which had parallels to my last relationship. There was no way on this earth I was ending up in the same situation again.

Learning to Love Myself

2017 was a dark year for me. I wasn't good. I didn't see the point in life. I didn't want to live. I certainly didn't want to be going into work and asking how everyone else was doing. My job required me to take care of everyone else's needs, which I really did not give a shit about. I did a good job at hiding how I was really doing. I went into robot mode. Had I not had the dog to get myself up in the morning to start my day, I don't think I would have made it into work at all. My beautiful Mr Boo. My born-blind Chow Chow. I had a responsibility to him. He was my purpose in life at that point. He needed me. I needed to take care of him.

I haven't introduced him. Mr Boo was my brother's ex-partners dog, and she paid a small fortune for him. £3000 pounds, to my understanding. At six months old she decided that he was too much effort. Leigh had gone up to visit the kids. Yes, Leigh has two boys by the same woman. He asked what the dog was doing out in the garden.

She said, 'Kids don't want it!' I think the oldest boy is allergic to Mr Boo's hair. She certainly didn't want it, had suggested that she would put him down! Leigh took the dog. Leigh loved the dog and Mr Boo loved, adored Leigh, but Mr Boo is a Chow Chow. He is a pure breed. He needs a lot of care, and you cannot be feeding him cheap biscuits from Poundland. Leigh didn't do it out of neglect, he just didn't know. Leigh phoned me up one day. 'Sis, I'm going to India to live.'

'What about the dog?'

'Umm, I'll find someone to take him.'

I immediately said, 'He can come and live with me.' Boo was a year old at that point.

When I was looking to move to Hawaii, I was going to look into ways to take him with me. I wasn't going to abandon him just like that. Mr Boo is my angel. He was my purpose in those dark days. The days that I spent in my room crying over that human whom I thought was the love of my life.

I threw myself into my training, and made sure that I was nurturing myself with food. Forcing myself to cook a meal every night. Treating myself with kindness and owning my feelings. Letting myself really feel what I was feeling. I didn't look to self-medicate. I thought the worst thing I could do was take drugs or drink alcohol. That was the last thing I wanted to do. Own them, feel them, work through them and hope that I would come out the other side real soon.

Rafael did eventually get around to contacting me, after I had written him a letter that was so angry and raw. I think I buried all my hurt feelings from back in the '90s when we were first together. I know I poured everything out into that letter. I let him have it!

It obviously pricked his attention, because he opened up the communication. We started to chat a bit. But it wasn't long before he started his stupid shit. He texted me, TEXTED ME, one morning to tell me that he was having questions about being together.

I asked him, 'OK, why?'

His response was MY BREASTS! Yes, you read it right, my breasts. They didn't satisfy him.

I said, 'You motherfucker, are you twelve years old! Fuck

me, I am a forty-six-year-old woman, what the fuck do you think they are going to look like?'

He suggested plastic surgery. I told him to get fucked. I am not doing that for anyone. If I would ever do it, it would be because I was doing it for myself.

I then facetimed him, fuck that texting shit, he needed to see my face. I was now shouting at him down the phone, 'You know there is a lot of shit about you that I am not satisfied with, but I love you in spite of them.' I continued to say, 'but now that we are on the subject let's have a conversation about them. Shall we have a talk about your dick that doesn't work! I didn't talk about it before because I didn't want to hurt your feelings, but now you have opened up the platform for discussion, let's talk about it. Oh, and another thing, your man boobs!'

That stupid fucker in his twenties had taken the wrong type of steroid to train with and grown moobs (man boobs), the dick! Now that he didn't train, they were really obvious.

I also told him that, 'When I say you look great, I'm just being nice, because it's a nice thing to do when you love someone. But motherfucker, you aren't that lean, and really, you could do with going to the gym.'

So that was that. It took me a while to sever the connection I had with him. I did torment him a little bit with sending him obnoxious postcards from different parts of the world I was visiting. It just made me chuckle. I knew it got to him, because he sent me an email to tell me to stop doing it. That pleased me to no end. We did not speak for about a year, and then he sent me an email to tell me that he still loved me, then did not contact me for around a month. Who does that? Maybe he was just playing a game with me?

The last time we spoke was a year ago. It was like watching

car crash T.V. As I watched him over Facetime down three or four bottles of beer before eight a.m. in the morning. I thought, 'What was I thinking! There isn't any amount of time in the world that is going to fix him. He also doesn't want to be fixed. He is happy dealing with his demons with drugs and alcohol.' I did love him. I don't love him any more.

I have ventured down the dating website journey looking for a new love, and it is horrendous. I have tried all the different websites as well. They are all awful. I met one guy for tea. I thought, 'I'll give him an hour during the day. That way he doesn't think that he is getting anything more than tea.' The small talk on these sites is soul-destroying. The messaging, the messaging over WhatsApp, it goes on and on and on... The pictures of weird shit, the dicks; some guy sent me a picture of him in the '90s as a bodybuilder. He's in his late 50s now. I mean, what the fuck? That picture is insignificant now.

I went and met tea boy. I turned up, and he was sat at the table with his own bottle of water.

I said, 'Hi.' He didn't get up. We sat for a moment, and I said, 'Are we getting tea?'

'Oh yes,' he said.

We walked over to the counter where he then asked if we can have an arm wrestle.

I looked at him with distain and say 'NO!' He then asked if he can touch my bicep. As he reached out to touch me, I smacked his hand away from me and said, 'There will be no touching!'

I gave him some of my time for tea, but, no. He was a fucking idiot. I fist-bumped him to say bye. No fucking chance boyo. He then messaged me later to tell me how fun and cool I am. I fucking know that, shit bag. I ignored his message. He then messaged me in the morning to say, 'Well I didn't think it went that bad.'

I messaged him back, 'I am already at work.' It was eight a.m. I also told him that, 'My best friend's mum is being taken off life support today, so I am a bit fucking busy!'

That put paid to that one.

Another guy I went to meet off the dating websites was from Weymouth. I drove from Bournemouth to Dorchester, which took about an hour. I thought 'What the hell, I'm up for an adventure.' I arrived first. He got out of his car and was walking like a fucking fridge-freezer. In my head I was like, 'What the fuck is going on there? Why is he limping so bad?'

I asked him, 'What's going on there then?'

'Knee surgery.'

'Right, OK'. Phew! I know, very shallow. But I am a really physically active woman. I'm not sure how it would work. Which is really bad of me, I know.

The date went well. The banter was good. We were getting on pretty well. It was now getting late. He said, 'Do you want to come back to mine for a chat?'

Code for he was working on me for a shag. I thought to myself, 'It is now close to midnight and it would be an hour home driving with me tired.' Or go back to his, NOT TO HAVE SEX and then I could drive home in the morning fresh. I said, 'Where do you live?'

'Fifteens mins down the road.'

'OK sure, but there will be no sex.'

I put the boundary out there. Now, I have spoken to a guy friend of mine who has said that I was a dick tease. But why can't I go back and just chat and sleep and not have sex. Why should that automatically mean that I am asking for it, or that I am dick teasing him? I set the boundary he could have quite easily have

226

sent me on my way.

We get to his house. We had a little cuddle on the sofa. He said, 'I'll sleep down here. You can sleep upstairs.'

I said, 'Look, we are both in our forties. Surely you can control yourself enough that we can sleep in the same bed?'

Again, my male mate said that I was still being a dick tease. How? Why can't you men control yourself. If a woman says no why can that not mean no?

He was up those stairs so fast and into that bed, covers pulled right up to his chin. He quick smart turned the lights off. I thought, 'Ahh, he thinks I'm shy, bless him.' I kept my underwear on and snuck into the bed.

He then proceeded to spend the whole night sticking his penis in my side, begging me to have sex.

'Please, please, please, please, please!'

'Dude, honestly, fucking control yourself, go to sleep!'

Now, I know, I went to a stranger's house. On my own. But really, a guy that was two stone lighter than me with a dodgy leg and did not lift a weight whatsoever. What was he going to do to me? I had already weighed that situation up in the bar on our date.

In the morning when we woke, he was knelt up in front of me, asking me, 'To finish him off!'

'Finish yourself off!' I mean, what! Finish him off, err…

I did however give him the benefit of the doubt. I did go for a second date, just in case I had misjudged him. I have these black skinny jean dungarees which I like. I had on my sexy tie-dye t-shirt on underneath. That's cute as well, no sleeves, open back, cuteness. Bright pink bra on underneath. I embrace the look and feel good when I have that outfit on. Off I trotted on our second date.

We went off and had some lunch at the local pub, getting

along pretty well again. He then asked me if I wanted to watch him play pool later on.

'Sure!'

'OK cool, we'll go get changed.'

'I don't have anything else with me!'

He then told me that I was never to wear the dungarees again!

What! I mean, what the actual fuck! Who the fuck is he to tell me what I can and cannot wear?

I informed him that if I came again that I would wear them every time I came and that I did not give a fuck about what he thought about them. I should have left there and then really. I stayed though, went and watched him play pool and then went back to his to stay.

He again was up those stairs quick smart again, undressed and into bed before I could see him undress. The lights were not for me, they were for him. He clearly did not want me to see him without his clothes on.

I didn't go back for a third date, idiot!

Internet dating websites are an inane cycle of mind-boring chatting and messaging. You have this person on your phone that you really know nothing about. You're getting excited about the messaging, to then only meet them in the flesh and know within the first five seconds that it is not going to work. IT IS SOUL-DESTROYING!

The last interlude that I went on was another guy that I met on one of the dating sites. His pictures were cool. He had one of him doing CrossFit and MMA. I thought, 'OK, that's cool. We have some common interests.' He also had one of him with a fish. What is it with men and putting up pictures of themselves holding a fish? Listen, MEN, all men. I cannot imagine there is a woman on this planet that is interested in your fish picture! Get rid!

We set up a date, and he took me bowling. I thought that was cool. We hit it off. The bants was good. He beat me at the bowling. You can't be great at everything! He then took me to Nando's after. The bants was still cool. On the drive home he asked if I wanted to go for coffee.

I said 'Sure.'

We were getting on really well. I invited him into my house. I told him that he had passed the test, so I didn't need to do him in (beat him up). He laughed and said that he had had the same thoughts. On the drive down to pick me up he had said to himself, 'She can outbox me and definitely will be stronger than me, but I can run faster than her!'

'Before we have a coffee, I need to take the dog for a quick walk. Do you want to come?'

'Sure'.

As he came into my room, he stood with his gob open! 'Wow, can I have one please?'

All my medals are out on show.

'NO! You cannot.'

He then looked at my bedside table and asked if those were nunchucks?

'Yes.'

'I think it might be a good idea to put them away.'

'I am a woman who lives on her own. I keep them by my bed, if anyone decides they are coming in my home, they will get them rapped around their heads!'

After the dog walk, we sat until about one a.m. just chatting away. 'I've got to get to bed.'

'Can I see you again?'

At that point I liked him. 'Sure.'

He then picked me up off my feet and kissed me hard. I thought, oh yes, oh yes, oh yes... Someone with a little something-something about them. Amazing!

We messaged each other for a week, he tells me what he's going to do to me. Candles, strip me down, blah, blah, blah.

We set up another date. Whilst the week has been exciting, him telling me what he's going to do to me, I had to tell him, 'Don't get your hopes up. I'm on my period, I'm at the end of my cycle. We'll just have to do all the sexy stuff next time.'

We had a lovely meal and went back to mine. He decided that he was staying the night, and we had a kiss and a cuddle. In the morning one thing led to another, and we had unprotected sex. He assumed that I wouldn't be able to get pregnant. He actually expressed that. His leaving comment was, 'Well, you won't be able to get pregnant!'

I did think, I'm not sure that's so true. I looked it up. A man's sperm can live in your vagina for up to seven days. If you are ovulating you will become pregnant.

I decided to leave that nugget of information until I saw him again.

We had another great date. He promised that he was going to do all this great sexy stuff with me over text. Could talk the talk but REALLY could not walk the walk! It turns out, that he could not get his kit off fast enough and get the duvet pulled right up to his neck. Where he then proceeded to put the durex on underneath the covers. I sat there and thought, 'This isn't what I had imagined. This isn't what he talked about in the messages.'

He then proceeded to just lay on his side and very slowly pump away. I thought, 'Christ, I am going to have to put on a performance with this one and get this finished up quick smart.' He, on the other hand, had his game face on! I needed to not be looking at his face. I whipped myself around, took up doggy

230

position and got that finished up!

While he was cleaning himself up, I said, 'You know your sperm can live in my womb for seven days?'

'What?'

'You know we had unprotected sex. Well, if I am ovulating, I could get pregnant.'

'Are you pregnant?'

'I don't feel it, but think we should have this conversation just in case.'

He laid down on the bed like rigor mortis had set in. Dead straight, arms by his sides. He was talking to me like it was my fault. Motherfucker, I can't do it on my own. He then asked if I would keep it.

I had to remind myself, I'm forty-six right. It was like I was having a conversation with a teenager.

'Probably, I'm forty-six years old. It's not like it's going to ruin my life!'

He laid there for a moment and this is what came out of his mouth!

'WHAT AM I GOING TO TELL MY MUM!'

The guy was thirty-nine years old. Another fucking douchebag. He got up, got dressed and left. Ran away!

I did not hear a peep from him for three months. Not even a phone call to see if I was OK.

It was bank holiday weekend. I had gone to the Bournemouth 7's festival, I was posting pics on social media. I was having an 'I look hot' time! You know those times when you just feel hundred per cent on it? I was out with Leigh as well, cute yellow hippy dress, looking fabulous, posting pics again. Who should pop up, but him. 'You look like you are having fun.'

'What do you want?'

He then told me was there is a thunder storm coming.

'Right, who made you weather man. Why the fuck did I need

231

to know that?'

'Wouldn't it be sexy doing 'IT' in a thunder storm?'

I said, 'Listen, you ran away!'

'What do you mean? You mean because of the pregnancy?'

'Yeah, you fucking ran away, you didn't even check in with me!'

'If you were pregnant, I thought I would be the first to know.'

'In my book that makes you a fucking dick!'

He tried to deflect the conversation by telling me that I looked hot.

'That's because I am hot motherfucker!'

He wanted to come and see me that night!

'No fucking way, you are going to have to put some work in, if you want to be with me again. You can take me out to dinner first.'

'OK, this Friday?'

'OK, sure.'

I waited. I did not hear from him for at least fifteen months, where he popped up on my Facebook with a friend request. I messaged him, 'What do you want?'

'I thought we were friends?'

'No, we are not.'

'But you are really cool, I would like to be friends.'

I always give people the benefit of the doubt. We chatted for a couple of days. I then reminded him of the dinner he still owed me. He told me I had a memory of an elephant and that he couldn't do that because he was SEEING SOMEONE and that it wouldn't be fair to her!

That motherfucker! Why was he trying to speak to me then? I blocked him from everything. What a prize-class twat.

That was the end of meeting men on the dating websites. I just cannot stand it. It is awful. I hate it. To me it is just desperate trying to meet desperate. I am not desperate and I will not just

232

make do because I feel lonely.

I have come to the point in my life now that if I meet someone, I meet someone. I will do this the organic way and not through scrolling through pictures on a dating website. It is so shallow; I can't stand it.

I have also realised that I was trying to find someone to love me. To fill the hole that has been missing my whole life from the lack of love not gained as a child. It has taken me a good thirty years to figure that one out. I am standing still, trying really hard to love myself, fill up my own hole. I'm appreciating the goodness of who I am, without tearing myself down and telling myself I am no good. I'm holding out hope that I will find a partner that will have the sensitivity to let me show all my scars and love me enough to accept all my insecurities.

After spending almost nine years at Bournemouth University, I graduated in 2017 with a master's by research; you can google me: "Janine Davis, ethnography." You'll find me. Have a read. Of all my achievements, that is my biggest one yet. I was told at fifteen, 'You are not clever enough to become a P.E. teacher.'

I held on to that for such a long time. I can do whatever I want now. I have spent over twenty years training, competing, educating and pushing myself. ON MY OWN.

You remember the lecturer that told me that I would not be able to do my master's? It turns out I sat next to her at my master's graduation. I had the best smug grin on my face while I was eating my little picnic that I took because graduations go on forever! In my head I was saying to myself, 'Fuck you, fuck you. I fucking did it and I passed it.' My research is there forever and ever. Janine Davis, an academic and world champion. As I stuffed my face, she prodded me with her PhD scroll and asked, 'What are you doing?'

'I'm eating, I'm hungry!'

She then responded that in all her years of doing graduations, she had never seen anyone get out a picnic.

'Well, more fool them. I'm hungry now and I am not waiting another three hours of clapping for people I don't know to get something to eat!'

Dad never came to see me get my master's. At that point our relationship had soured. It always does, because he can't keep up the façade for very long. I had never told him about Rafael and the fact that he had HIV, but a situation had arisen where I needed to tell him or else he was going to hear it from someone else. He and my sister made a really big deal out of it. One hundred percent judged me for it. My sister stopped me from coming and seeing her and the kids because I had spent time with a person living with HIV. I told her in no uncertain terms exactly what I thought about that. So ignorant and uneducated!

My dad decided all of a sudden that he was going to start parenting me! I mean, what a fucking joke! Number one, he doesn't know who I am as a person. Number two, he is as thick as shit when it comes to his education around HIV and how you can contract it. I sat there on Facetime having to educate him on it and how I had done my own research and that he needed to fucking do one with the parenting speech. I was forty-six years old. I certainly didn't need a speech from him now, especially when he had no educational grounds to preach to me. So, that was that. He certainly wasn't going to come and see me graduate, neither him or Mum has ever seen or been to anything that I have achieved. Well fuck them both!

I am a better person without them.

Leigh phoned me one day in 2018 and said, 'Sis, do you want to hear a funny story?'

If it's from my brother, it's going to be funny.

'Definitely!'

Leigh's Story

Leigh phoned me when he was twenty-one. 'Sis, I've got a girl pregnant!'

'OK, we'll go meet the parents of the girl and figure out how we are going to move forwards.'

The girl was a party girl. She had to decide out of three guys who the father was. She figures it was Leigh's.

I told him, 'You are not going to do what Dad did to us. You are going to do the right thing and be there for that kid.'

Leigh tried to have a relationship with this girl. It turned out that Leigh's relationship with this girl had parallels to his relationship with Mum. There was a lot of verbal abuse. Putting him down, trying to control him. He wasn't even allowed to watch pretty women on the T.V. She also wanted another child; Leigh was opposed to it, but she tricked him into thinking she was on the pill and got her pregnant.

The relationship did not last. Leigh got out. Leigh is the freest spirit you will ever meet. You will never tie him down.

This girl was a glamour model when he met her. Unbeknownst to him, she had got into being an escort. He found out because he was at her house looking after the boys whilst she was away in Dubai apparently being a VIP hostess. Leigh had found CDs and her website promoting herself as a prostitute. Leigh was gutted. At one point Leigh had loved her. But he could just not get his head around being with her and her sleeping with other men for a living. Along with the fact that she had lied about what she was doing.

Leigh under the circumstances did the best job that he could do at being the boys' dad. She definitely pulled all the strings and used the kids against him. She still thinks to this day that they will end up together and will stop at nothing to get at Leigh and hurt him.

When he phoned me to tell me the funny story, they were in a place of possibly figuring things out. He had told her to go away, travel and find herself. Get new friends, find a new life, stop the prostitution.

She had up to this point befriended my dad. She was travelling backwards and forwards to USA prostituting herself out there. The boys would be left with whomever whilst she went from state to state earning her money. My dad had let her use his address so that she could get a bank account. I did tell him to be careful with that, because obviously that money was not being earned legally and he was still not a citizen of the USA, even though he has lived there for over thirty years (fucking useless!).

He dismissed it and they carried on as is. She would post pictures of herself on Facebook, her lips being pumped up looking like a twat or other sexy type pictures and my dad would gush over them. It was sickening. My dad is the kind of man that constantly post pictures of women's tits and their asses. He has that 1970s misogynistic attitude towards women. I told him that I was a sports therapist. He said, 'Oh yeah, you give happy endings?'

I looked at him and thought, 'I am your fucking daughter!' No, I don't give happy endings you fucking twat.

Let's call the girl Linda. Leigh's Linda was not away finding herself. She was in America, clearly prostituting again. Apparently, she had had a heart attack of some sorts and did not feel well. Her mum called my dad and asked if he would go and check on her. My dad drove out of his way to pick her up and then they went on a four-day camping trip together. My dad was hard-pressed to spend two days with me. He was also super happy for me to spend ten hours in an airport on my own. But he can go on a four-day camping trip with this fucking asshole.

I tried to talk Leigh down. The story was not really a funny story at all. He was beside himself.

He said, 'I fucking know her!' At this point she had been a prostitute for over twenty years. Leigh in that time had found out that she was doing up to ten men a day! I mean, good for her; she has bought a £450,000.00 house for herself. But at what cost to her soul?

When you have been a prostitute for that long, a penis is a penis is a penis. One more with whomever it is; old, young, a dad, I am sure will not matter.

I said, 'Leigh, I don't think dad would do that,' and that he was just taking care of her. I mean, it is pretty sad really, she has no friends and is hanging out with our dad'.

Leigh settled down, and believed what I had said to him. I did think that Dad might have called him.

Leigh called me two days later. 'Do you want round two?'

'Sure, give it to me.'

He was talking to Linda about one of the boys over Facetime. The youngest was going to be staying with Leigh in India. Yes, Leigh lives in India most of the year now. They were talking for at least fifteen to twenty minutes.

Now, if you know my dad, he is not one to sit there silent. When Leigh got off the phone, he thought, 'She is in the car with someone.' He phoned her back, and asked her 'who she was in the car with?'

237

She turned the phone around; it was my dad! Dad couldn't look him in the eye. He looked straight out of the window. He then looked back and said, 'Oh hi son, we are just looking for a cash point.'

My heart sank. 'Oh Leigh!' I couldn't at that point justify Dad's behaviour of what the both of them were up to. I did say, 'Leigh we have no proof. But the way that Dad has handled this whole situation makes it look very bad.'

Leigh was destroyed. That was the final straw for him. That was the relationship severed. We don't talk about it; he never wants Dad's name mentioned ever!

I hadn't actually spoken to Dad around that time. As far as he was aware I wouldn't even know about it. I went looking for him on Facebook around three months later. I couldn't find him. I thought, 'That's strange.' I asked, 'Leigh is Dad on your Facebook?'

'No, he's blocked me.'

I then asked his brother, my uncle, but he said, 'No, we are not speaking.' That's a whole other issue, not one to get into now. I then thought, 'I know, I'll ask Cassandra.' I messaged her and said, 'You still friends with my dad on Facebook?'

'Yes, he was on about twenty minutes ago.'

I thanked her, and then thought, 'That motherfucker has blocked me! '

I messaged Sarah, his wife. I thought, 'I bet she doesn't know that he's been on a four-day camping trip with a prostitute.' I said to Sarah, 'I'm trying to find Dad.'

She said, 'Oh, I don't know about Facebook.'

It turns out that he has blocked her as well for a separate incident. The guy is a child. She said, 'But he's here asleep. I said, 'Cool, tell him to contact me when he wakes up, please.'

I then sent him an email, to tell him that if he did not get in contact with me there were going to be consequences to his actions. I had decided that I would tell Sarah about his trip if he did not contact me.

It took him a couple of days. The first call I ignored on purpose because I just wasn't ready yet to speak to him. The next time he called it was ten p.m. at night for me, I was just getting myself ready for bed. I thought, 'Do I, don't I?' Answer it, that is.

'Hello.'

'Hey Janine,' in his stupid American English accent. 'Hey Janine, Oh I am so busy with work, blah, blah, blah, blah…'

'OK, cut the shit. Why did you block me?'

Ahh, oh, ahh… I don't know, I must have done it as a family thing!'

What an absolute crock of shit. If anyone is on Facebook, you know how to block people! You have to type the name in. It then asks you if you are sure you want to block this person. You then have to click, OK and then it blocks. You certainly cannot set it as a block family book.

I thought, 'Whatever!' I didn't care about his response at that point. I wanted to call him out on it and to let him know that I knew. Such a coward.

'OK,' I said, moving on. 'What's going on with Linda? You know she has been pretty awful to Leigh over the years.'

'That's none of my business.'

'Leigh is your son, where is your loyalty?'

'I didn't think he wanted anything to do with her?'

And? What does that matter? I couldn't believe what I was hearing. The true behaviour, completely exonerate yourself of any responsibility to being a father. As far as he was concerned,

239

Linda was fair game.

I told him Leigh's emotional welfare was of the utmost importance to me. I had been there for him. I had been Mum, Dad, everything for Leigh. I would also do anything I need to do to protect him.

Dad became very defensive at that point. He started shouting down the phone. He told me that he would not be told by anyone who he could and could not hang out with.

I then told him, 'Let's get one thing straight: you have done exactly what you wanted to do with your life. You have never taken responsibility for anything.'

His response to that was, 'Well, Leigh's soon on the phone when he wants something!' I thought, 'You are his fucking Father, what the fuck is wrong with you?'

I told him that the way he handled the situation was completely wrong and that he needed to fix it. I then also told him that I would knock him the fuck out if he ever hurt Leigh!

'I know.'

The call ended; we have never spoken since.

My next conversation with Leigh was, 'I am done. I am forty-six years old. I cannot put up with this shit any more. I do not want these people in my life. Useless, pointless, toxic people, that bring nothing to our lives. It is done and it is over.'

Life as It Is Now

I found out just before the pandemic hit in 2020. Dad came to the UK in February 2020. He went to see Linda and then drove down past Bournemouth to Tavistock to see his brother. Did he stop to see me? That would be a NO. Such a coward. You cannot pick your family and you certainly cannot pick who you are born to. Me and Leigh had the misfortune of not just having one bad parent, but two. Mum unfortunately has mental health issues. Dad, well Dad is not a dad. He hasn't earnt the right to be called Dad.

That's OK, though. I am working hard on finding the love inside of me. It's taken me nearly fifty years to figure that out. But, instead of trying to fill the hole with someone else, I am trying to do it myself. Nurture, self-love and kindness. Knowing my worth. The saddest part of my journey so far in my life is that I have never had anyone who loves me. My friends love me of course, but that's not the same as unconditional love. I do not know what it means to be loved. When I think about it sometimes, I am sad. But then, that is life, and you have to make shit work for you. I would like to meet someone before I die that truly accepts me for me.

Leigh, well, he is flying high. He's always on an adventure. Leigh is a true free spirit. He lives most of his time in Goa, in India. He loves it out there. I think he has truly found his peace out there. He tries to be the best Dad he can be with the tools that he has. The one thing he has done is always been there. Not material wealth, but physical wealth when he is back in the country. He certainly doesn't just call once a year to mend his own guilt.

I like to look back on each year and see what I have achieved. I want to make sure that I am always pushing myself and looking for new opportunities to step outside of my comfort zone.

My sporting adventure now is with CrossFit, which is tough! It is pushing me to move my body in a way that I would have never done on my own. My right knee will definitely have a shelf life. It is hanging on by a thread now. The fourth operation really finished it off. It will not stop me though; I just try to work around the pain and managing my expectations of what it is able to do.

I took up sea swimming three years ago, which I love. All year round. No wetsuit. The winter time, whilst absolutely baltic and six degrees Celsius is the coldest I have been in. I am one hundred percent addicted to it. You take so much for your wellbeing from being in the ocean. At some point I am looking to swim the channel.

I'm not sure what the next adventure will be, but I am sure something will pop up for me to do and sink my teeth into. Grab life by the balls and never give in.

I was working as a P.E. teacher in a school with children that have autism in 2021. A friend of mine who decided that he could do a better job than anyone else had the balls to open up his own school. I did love it. It was challenging, rewarding and exhausting. I did finally become a P.E. teacher. Unfortunately, you cannot control the people you work with, and I am in a place now that I will not tolerate any kind of abusive behaviour towards me, big or small. I had to leave. Which is sad, because I really loved what I was doing.

No matter though, I am still very successful with my

personal training business and still have new clients all the time that want train with me twenty years on.

Nothing in this life is easy to come by. I am still fighting the fight at fifty. Life will throw all kinds of challenges at you. You need to get up every day, put those fighting gloves on and never give in. With hard work and dedication, you can achieve anything you want to achieve. I would love to visit that careers advisor that spoke to me when I was fifteen and show her everything that I have done. Fuck you. I AM clever enough.

I am not about to compromise on who I am. I am who I am. I am strong, opinionated, powerful, intelligent, independent and super funny. Aggressive? NO. Do I have a voice? Yes! Am I afraid to be me? NO. All the attributes that still go against the grain of what it means to be a woman.

I wouldn't have it any other way!